Sydney Opera House

Phaidon Press Ltd
Regent's Wharf
All Saints Street
London N1 9PA

Phaidon Press, Inc
180 Varick Street
New York, NY 10014

www.phaidon.com

First published 1995
Reprinted 1999
This edition first published 2002
© 1995, 2002 Phaidon Press Limited

ISBN 0 7148 4215 X

A CIP catalogue record for this book
is available from the British Library.

Library of Congress Cataloguing In
Publication Data available.

Printed in Hong Kong

Sydney Opera House
Jørn Utzon

Philip Drew
ARCHITECTURE IN DETAIL

1

2

4

1, 2 Sydney Harbour, view towards Sydney Harbour Bridge and Circular Quay with ferry wharves from west.

3 Jørn Utzon with the early model of the Opera House.

4 The Sydney Opera House introduces the city from the water. The wall of CBD towers behind the Cahill Expressway is framed on either side by two ridges, Macquarie Street and the Sydney Harbour Bridge.

3

A highly visible symbol

It is hard to believe, a quarter of a century later, that Jørn Utzon was prevented from finishing his great work by a little known politician from the country. One thing that stands out today with startling clarity is how misinformed the journalists and conservative politicians of the day were. Their exaggerated predictions of failure of the Opera House now seem ludicrous. The Sydney Opera House is one of the truly great buildings of the world: two out of three readers of *The Times* in Britain and the *Australian* placed it first in their list of the Seven Wonders of the Modern World in 1992, and it is the leading tourist attraction in New South Wales. A symbol, not only of Sydney, but of Australia,[1] its distinctive zig-zag arc roof was adopted for the successful Sydney 2000 Olympic logo.

By forcing Utzon to leave, Minister Davis Hughes achieved a dubious kind of notoriety in precipitating, in critic Robert Hughes' words, 'one of the bitterest cultural traumas Australia had ever experienced'.[2]

Today it is impossible to think of Sydney without, at the same time, bringing to mind its Opera House – indeed it can be said to be to Sydney what Notre Dame is to Paris. Moored to the banks of the River Seine by its bridges, Victor Hugo likened the Ile de la Cité, on which Notre Dame stands, to a great ship embedded in the mud. The Opera House is similar, a marvellous symbol constructed at a time of unprecedented economic boom; so exposed, so visible, so central, moored to Bennelong Point. Sydney was settled from the sea at the end of the eighteenth century; it is a maritime city split by the invading sea. And the Opera House is such an effective symbol of this city precisely because it carries so many sea images in its cargo.

The decision to build an opera house, particularly the choice of Utzon's scheme, marked an important cultural watershed which stands at the divide in the changeover from an older British Australia that was in decline, to an increasingly diverse European multi-cultural Australia. The Opera House set the tone for Sydney's ascendency over Melbourne and other Australian capitals; and, at $102 million, it was a colossal bargain.[3] It is easy to forget what a fluke the Sydney Opera House was; it happened, despite apathy and the political and newspaper attacks, because the very idea behind it was so appropriate. Utzon gave Sydney a visible symbol. Building it challenged the notion that Australians were a nation of beerswilling gamblers, more interested in footy than the arts. Today the position is reversed: more people in Australia visit art galleries and attend concerts than go to sports events.

As a decade, the fifties was more complex than we tend to acknowledge. It was characterized by many things, often in opposition. It feared the spread of Communism, and this was the source of much paranoia that stained the open and generous spirit of the time. Yet, in spite of its extreme conservatism it did allow things to happen, many of which would be impossible today. The Sydney Opera House was one. By the time conservative Australia woke up to what was happening it was too late. John Joseph Cahill, Premier of New South Wales, knew this, which is why he pushed the project forward and was in such a hurry to have the Opera House built.

The 1950s looked forward to a better world and aspired to cultural improvement as the counterpart of a rising standard of living. The Sydney Opera House is emblematic of this post-war longing for change – a naive reaching out for culture without quite understanding what was involved. Only in Australia could anything so daring as Jørn Utzon's Opera House have been attempted.

The Sydney Opera House is now embedded in Sydney's consciousness. Many factors have made it the popular symbol it undoubtedly is – the Opera House Lotteries, the controversy over the design, the intense media coverage at every step along the way, each in some way assisted. It represented something important to many people, opening their minds to hopes denied them by a world war and the depression, and the wish for a greater opportunity to enjoy life. It symbolized a more cultured way of life and touched people's hearts.[4] Little wonder, then, that it has become such a potent representation of Sydney, or that so many ordinary people still care very much what happens to it.

5

5 Aerial view from southwest.
The Sydney Opera House is
the jewel in Sydney's harbour-
crown. Overseas Passenger
Terminal in the foreground.
6 Sketch by Utzon to
accompany the Opera House
competition scheme.

Eugene Goossens – the musical vision
The driving force behind the Sydney
Opera House was Eugene Goossens,
conductor of the Sydney Symphony
Orchestra. He was supported by a few key
people such as the Labor politician J J
Cahill, and the Professor of Architecture at
the University of Sydney, H Ingham
Ashworth. But the musical vision alone
belonged to Goossens. In order to grasp
what the Sydney Opera House means
it is first necessary to understand
Goossens' aims.

Sir Eugene Goossens (1893–1962) was
a British violinist, conductor and
composer, whose family roots were in the
Flemish town of Bruges in Belgium.[5] Prior
to taking up the post of conductor at
Sydney he had been conductor of the
Rochester Philharmonic Orchestra and
the Cincinatti Symphony Orchestra, in
the United States. Goossens believed
unreservedly that music is the birthright
of the people, not the property of a small
group of initiates or a privileged few. His
mission was to bring music of the highest
quality to the mass of ordinary people, and
he looked forward to the day when great
orchestras would travel from town to town
and play full-sized programmes of the
greatest music in halls seating
3,000–4,000 people. Goossens wanted
music to reach out to people, and the
Sydney Opera House was only
a beginning in achieving this. This helps
to explain why Goossens felt such a large
main hall was needed.

Soon after he arrived in Sydney,
Goossens began advocating a
performance centre for music. He was
appointed conductor of the Sydney
Symphony Orchestra in 1946, and made
Director of the Conservatorium of Music
the following year. In July 1947 he called
for the provision of 'a fine concert hall for
the orchestra with perfect acoustics and
seating for 3,500 people, a home for
an opera company, and a smaller hall for
chamber music.'[6] Goossens considered
that such a centre would focus the
international spotlight of culture on
Sydney, and feared that without it
Australians would stagnate in outer
darkness. There was great urgency in his
plea to make a start as soon as possible.
In a radio talk the same year, Goossens
raised the subject of a war memorial opera
house for Sydney, an idea which
originated from a suggestion by the
consultant planner of the Cumberland
County Council, Dr K Langer, who had
included it in his proposals for
architectural additions to Sydney's cultural
life. Like the San Francisco War Memorial
Opera House which inspired it, it was
envisaged that the halls would be used for
both symphony concerts and opera. In a
subsequent statement, in October 1948,
Goossens insisted: 'it must furnish a home
for our symphony orchestra, opera, ballet
and choral festivals … The auditorium
must accommodate from 3,500–4,000 –
no fewer'.[7]

6

7

As a description, the term 'opera house' is misleading. The proposed Sydney Opera House was really a performing arts centre. Performing arts centres with dual-use auditoria were a product of the fifties, driven by the rationalist expectation that bringing together the performing arts under one roof would prove more economical than having them function separately. These centres grouped together an extraordinary range of musical and theatrical entertainments, including the performance of symphonic orchestral works, chamber music, opera, ballet and experimental drama. The aim was greater efficiency, the pooling of administration and support facilities. Their success ultimately depended upon the satisfactory acoustical design of auditoria for dual-use. In practice, however, dual-use compromised acoustic standards.

The first hurdle was the choice of a site. Goossens chose Bennelong Point in his 1948 announcement. His decision was reinforced in 1951 when the fifth year architecture students at the University of Sydney designed an opera house for Bennelong Point with Goossens acting as client.[8]

John Joseph Cahill was Minister for Local Government when the plan for an opera house was first presented to the Cumberland Council. It was Cahill who, on becoming Premier in 1952, announced that Sydney needed an opera house and arranged for a public meeting on 30 November 1954 to discuss the idea which led to the setting up of a committee.[9] Six months later, in May 1955, this committee recommended Bennelong Point as the site, with two halls seating 3,500 and 1,200 people, and that an international competition be held to select a suitable design. The terms for the design competition were announced in January. From the outset, therefore, the Sydney Opera House was identified with Cahill personally.

Four architects, Ingham Ashworth, Professor of Architecture at the University of Sydney, and originally from Manchester; Cobden Parkes, the New South Wales government architect; Dr Leslie Martin, the designer of the Royal Festival Hall in London; and Eero Saarinen, one of the leading names in contemporary architecture in the United States, were chosen to act as assessors. The aim of the competition was to select an architect and a design, and the programme's main emphasis was on the two halls, a Major Hall for symphony concerts and large-scale opera and ballet seating between 3,000–3,500 persons, and a smaller Minor Hall for drama, intimate opera and chamber music to seat 1,200 persons. The 25-page booklet prepared for the competition listed the requirements in order of importance,[10] including other additional requirements for an experimental theatre, orchestra rehearsal room, chamber music room, restaurant to seat 250 persons, meeting rooms, foyers and the like.

It was a lot to ask. No one seems to have doubted that the dual-function could be achieved with reasonably good acoustics for both uses, provided that the hall was adapted to meet the acoustical requirements for each. It should, however, have been obvious that a dual-purpose hall could not be expected to achieve the same level of perfection as a single-purpose hall. The size of the Major Hall followed the dubious practice in the United States where 3,000 was the average number of seats, compared to Europe where 1,400 was more usual. The smaller size of concert halls in Europe encouraged the most important acoustical attribute: acoustical intimacy; while the cubic volume of these smaller European opera houses was low enough to allow singers to fill the space without straining their voices. Today in the nineties, new opera halls at Lyon, Gothenburg, and Brussels are designed in the intimate Italian style with 1,300-, 1,250- and 1,200-seat capacities respectively.

8 Model of the Opera House, east elevation, competition scheme, 1957.
9 Slightly later model showing north elevation, Major and Minor Halls, at Utzon's studio in Hellebaek, Denmark, September 1960.

7

8

9

9 Opera House south elevation from the forecourt with entrances and main staircase. Competition scheme, c late 1956.
10 Kronborg Castle, Helsingør, 1574– (rebuilt 1629), a fortified palace begun for Frederick II which encloses a medieval castle.
11 Bennelong Point viewed from the west, here depicted in Jacob Janssen's painting *Sydney Cove*, 1842.

10

11

Despite the complexity of the brief, the competition attracted enormous interest internationally: 933 architects registered and 230 submitted designs. Judging took place in January 1957, and on 29 January Premier Cahill announced Danish architect Jørn Utzon as the winner. The assessors' statement seemed to anticipate some of the difficulties that lay ahead: '[Utzon's] drawings submitted for this scheme are simple to the point of being diagrammatic. Nevertheless, as we have returned again and again to the study of these drawings, we are convinced that they present a concept for an Opera House which is capable of becoming one of the great buildings of the world. We consider this scheme to be the most original and creative submission. Because of its very originality it is clearly a controversial design. We are, however, absolutely convinced about its merits …'

Irrespective of whether the story that Eero Saarinen arrived late and pulled Utzon's scheme from a pile of discarded drawings rejected by the other assessors is a true account, it nevertheless highlights how unexpected and controversial was the choice, at the same time making it abundantly clear that it was Saarinen's enthusiasm which was decisive. The assessors, perhaps anticipating criticism, added: '… we are aware that it is open to many points of detailed criticism and a number of corrections would have to be made'.

Importance of the site
At Sydney Heads, the Pacific Ocean smashes its way through towering sandstone cliffs and kicks sharply southwest; then some distance in, in front of Shark Island, its axis turns north-of-west passing under the Harbour Bridge, at which point the harbour is less than 500m wide. The Opera House is on the south or city side. Running down Bennelong ridge to the point roughly at right angles, the civic and political axis of government, Macquarie Street, finishes in front of the Opera House. A painting by Jacob Janssen[11] from 1842 captures the maritime atmosphere of Bennelong Point: the foreground is of crowded ship masts and rigging; Fort Macquarie (1817–1901) sits off the tip of Bennelong Point separated by a narrow channel; beyond the picturesque outline of the fort a succession of peninsulas dive into the water in quick succession as the eye moves down the harbour. In fact, the purpose of Fort Macquarie and its 24-pounders was to prevent clandestine departures.

Colonial Sydney was built in a hollow between two ridges – a west ridge which was higher, and a lower east ridge at Bennelong Point. This topography turned the city in a northeast direction so that it faces the harbour entrance. The early public buildings were located on these ridges to take advantage of the elevation and this accentuated the terrain. The containment of the early city along its sides, and the alignment of the main streets running back from the Cove forced the city to gravitate towards the water. Bennelong Point was first of all a naval control point, and later, after a large ugly shed was built in 1901 for the new electric trams, it became a transport terminus.

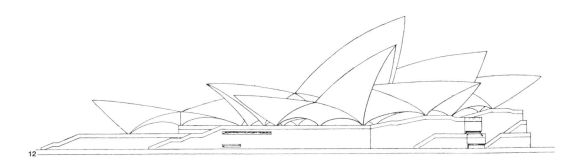
12

Because the harbour is constricted at Dawes Point and closed off by the Harbour Bridge, Bennelong Point is visible from many angles. Indeed, it is this extreme visibility which gives it its importance.

When Jørn Utzon came to design his Opera House in 1956, he began by studying sea charts of Sydney Harbour; from these he measured distances to assess the height of the surroundings to develop a feel for the landscape.[12] To further assist himself in visualizing the site, Utzon went to Helsingor, near his home at Hellebaek and looked out across the water from the great terrace: 'I stood looking at the clouds over a low coastline and I had a look at Kronborg Castle at Elsinore, and at Gothic churches. There you have forms against a horizontal line like the sea or the clouds without a single vertical line, nothing constituting weight, and with forms that are different from all angles.'[13] The genesis of the Sydney Opera House is thus found here in Utzon's account of his visit to Kronborg Castle. The Castle stands at the inlet to the Baltic sea between Denmark and Sweden. Its fanciful Renaissance turrets and stepped gables command Øre Sound, while in front is a magnificent grassed terrace. Ships passing through were obliged by Kronborg's cannons to pay a toll on their cargos. And, like Bennelong point, the castle was strategically situated.

The Aalto inheritance

The main sources of the Opera House design can be traced to Utzon's family upbringing and professional training; to the influence of his naval architect father who was the director of the local shipyard at Alborg.[14] His father was a brilliant yacht designer who had been trained in England early in the century.[15] Indeed, several of Utzon's family were yachtsmen. Utzon himself was a good sailor and was at first inclined to a career as a naval officer. He often visited his father's shipyard during his years at high school and helped by drawing up the plans for new types of yachts and making models.

This exposure to shipbuilding techniques gave Utzon the confidence that anything that was sensibly designed could be produced. It also directed Utzon's focus in the realization of buildings towards the use of models, prototypes and prefabrication. Moreover, Einar Utzon-Frank, his father's cousin, was a sculptor and professor at the Royal Academy of Fine Arts who encouraged Utzon to sculpt.

In 1937 Utzon was accepted at the School of Architecture of the Royal Academy of Fine Arts in Copenhagen where he studied under Kay Fisker and Steen Eiler Rasmussen, completing his thesis in 1942. During the Second World War, from 1942–5, he worked in Stockholm in the offices of Paul Hendquist and Gunnar Asplund. He was especially impressed by Gunnar Asplund (1885–1940), notably by his Woodland Crematorium at Stockholm and the Courthouse at Gothenburg.[16] For Utzon, Asplund had the gift of creating a wonderful feeling of well-being in his buildings. The big roof of the open hall of the Crematorium and the contrast of the white marble buildings set against evergreen pine trees, left their traces on the Opera House.

12 East elevation of the Opera House, competition drawing, reproduced in Utzon's *Yellow Book*.
13 Aerial view from the south shows the processional approach from forecourt to main staircase and podium with the Major and Minor Halls (Concert Hall and Opera Theatre) side by side and the Bennelong Restaurant in front.
14 Erik Gunnar Asplund, Woodland Crematorium, Stockholm, 1935–40, principal elevation showing chapels and Monument Hall

13

14

15

16

15 Concert Hall seating used a purpose-designed white birch veneer shell with magenta wool fabric covers.
16 Concert Hall, south foyer.
17 Looking west: Concert Hall ribbed vault with the Sydney Harbour Bridge in the distance.
18 Concert Hall foyer shell, east elevation.

The architecture of Alvar Aalto was also a deep influence on Utzon, and the source of many of the ideas behind the Sydney Opera House. In 1982 Utzon spoke of his debt to the Finnish architect: 'His example of the branch of the cherry blossoms with each blossom different from its neighbours according to its special position on the branch, but all the blossoms composed of the same elements, was a great eye-opener to me, and these ideas have been the foundation of many of my own projects.'[17] Utzon spent a year with Aalto in 1946. It is not easy to summarize all that Utzon carried away with him from Helsinki; instead it is easier to point to specific factors such as the thirties' Artek plywood furniture which

shaped his choice of plywood at the Sydney Opera House for the glass wall mullions and the moulded ceiling troughs; or his interest in visual screens where space is allowed to flow through in much the same way that the stair balustrade does in the living room of the Villa Mairea at Noormarkku. Utzon had a similar aim in his glass walls at the Opera House. The terrace was also an important element in Aalto's work; Aalto pushed the contours into terraces that extend the influence of the architecture out into the landscape. Utzon had encountered similar ideas in Frank Lloyd Wright and Mayan temples. His interest in maintaining the natural qualities of building materials derived from a wider Scandinavian heritage although Aalto probably sharpened his appreciation.

Aalto had explained his approach to mass-produced components with the phrase 'little sister of the columns'; Utzon, likewise, used 'mother cylinder' to describe the generating principle for his auditorium ceilings. The idea of a family of elements which combined to enclose spaces was a special preoccupation which gave rise later to the concept 'additive architecture'.[18]

Jørn Utzon – the architectural vision

'… instead of making a square form, I have made a sculpture – a sculpture covering the necessary functions, in other words, the rooms express themselves, the size of the rooms is expressed in these roofs. If you think of a Gothic church, you are closer to what I have been aiming at.

Looking at a Gothic church, you never get tired, you will never be finished with it – when you pass around it or see it against the sky. It is as if something new goes on all the time and it is so important – the interplay is so important that together with the sun, the light and the clouds, it makes a living thing.'[19]

The Sydney Opera House composition is based on the simple opposition of three groups of interlocking shell vaults and a heavy terraced platform. The two halls were arranged side by side and their longitudinal axes inclined very slightly so that they meet at the base of the concourse. This accommodated the wedge shapes of the halls. The auditoria were scooped out of the high north end of the podium platform like Greek theatres in order that they face south, with the stage areas between them and the main foyers.

Theatre-goers reach their seats from the forecourt at the south end by climbing a grand 86m (282ft) wide staircase of granite. Two flights of stairs separate the main terrace level from the forecourt. The Opera House can also be entered from under the 49m deep elevated concourse; from here, visitors are led up through the podium by three stairs connecting this lower level with the hall lobbies and the restaurant.

17

18

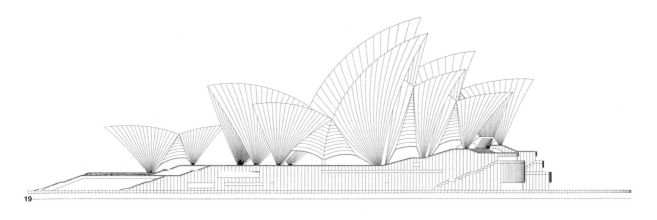

19

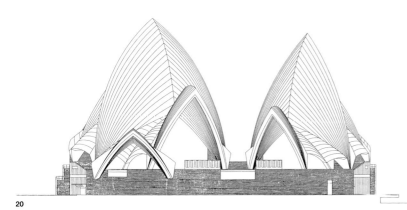

20

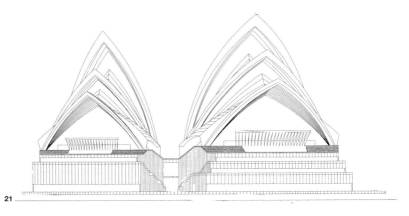

21

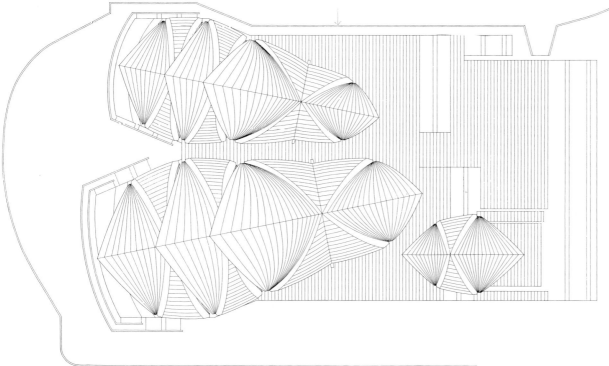

22

19–22 Drawings from Utzon's *Yellow Book*: east, south and north elevations (19, 20, 21 respectively), and site plan (22).

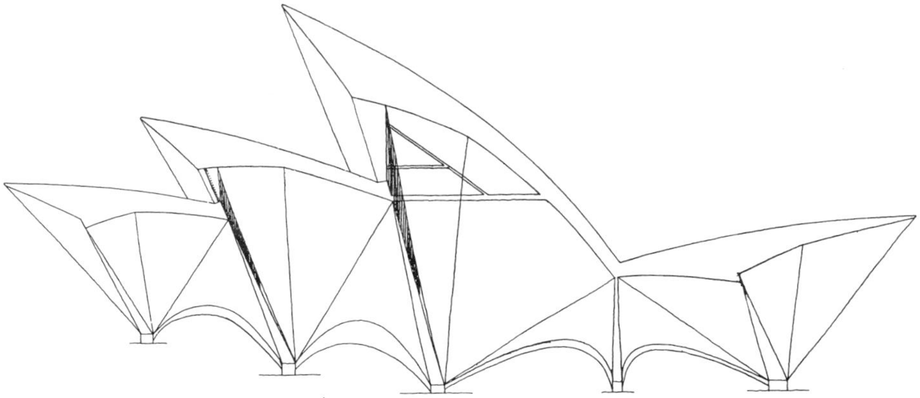

23

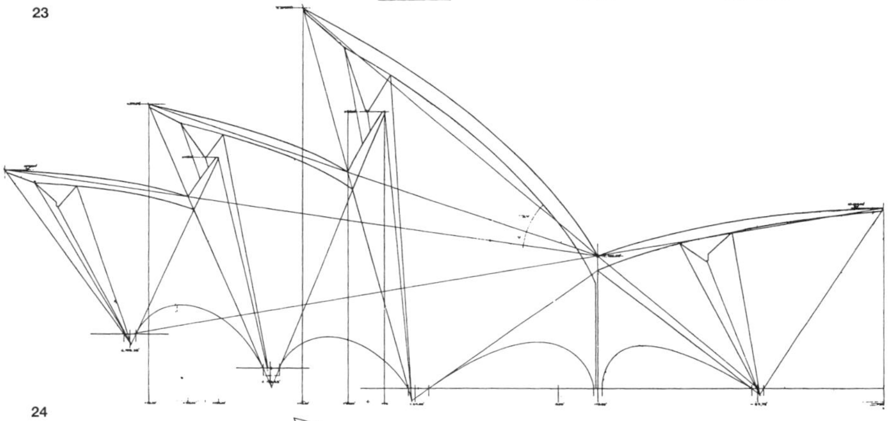

24

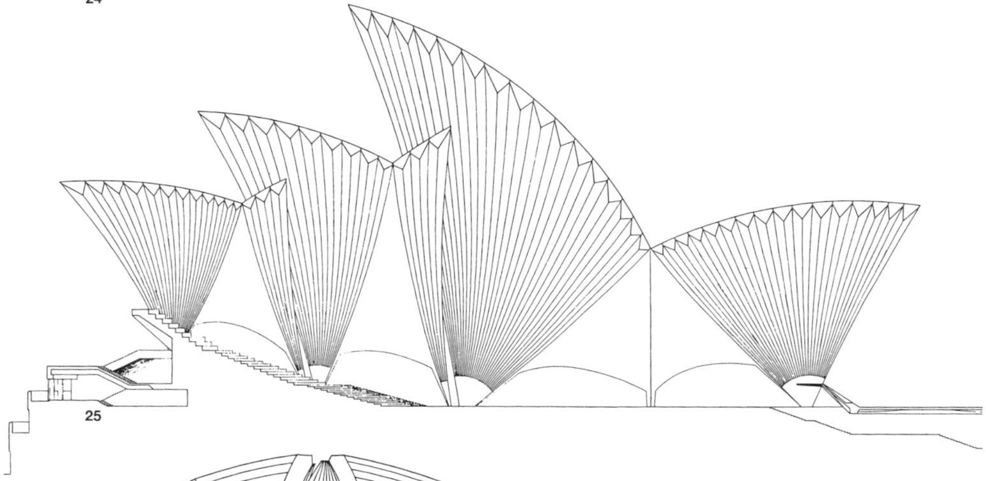

25

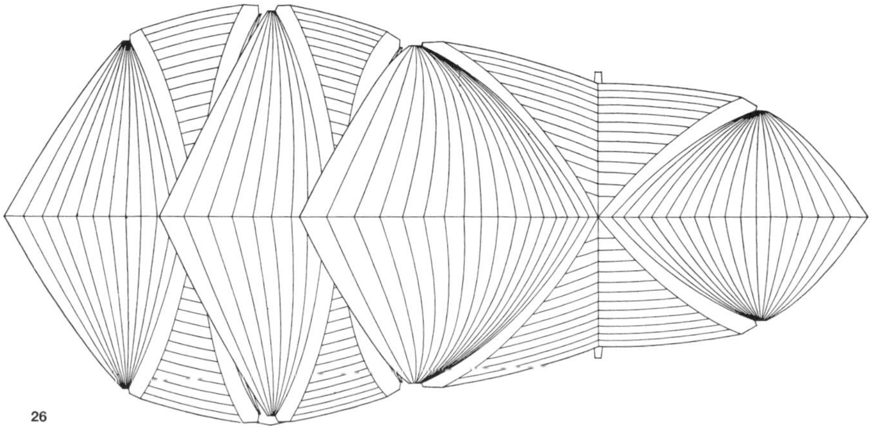

26

12   **23–26** *Yellow Book* drawings showing the development of the Opera House shells. Note the section through the Major Hall where ribs and vaults meet at one point (25, 26).

The Opera House roof was of major importance as it could be seen from above and from every side; Utzon called it the 'fifth facade' for this very reason. The competition design was based on the presumption of thin concrete shells about 5cm thick. These were low and in pairs that leaned against one another for stability; the space between was infilled by smaller shell segments. The structural scheme was diagrammatic. The shells' size was dictated by the volume of the rooms beneath, hence the Major Hall had quite a small shell over the southern foyer.

Much comment was directed at Utzon's omission of side and rear stages to handle scene changes. Utzon instead provided lifts under the stages so that scene changes could be made similar to the way in which aircraft are lifted onto the deck of a modern aircraft carrier; rather than making the scenery changes in the customary horizontal way, this would occur vertically. For Utzon, the Opera House would always be the 'house of festivals'; he distinguished between, on the one hand, activities taking place in the base, the mechanical parts of the theatre, the singers and musicians, stage hands and costumers, as well as the large workshops where all the sets and props were made; and, on the other, the patrons' areas, the festival side of things, where people would move freely without encountering, or even being aware of these other activities. This neatly divided the building into two parts: the *served* (auditoria and lobby) and *servant* spaces (kitchens, stage machinery, dressing and practice rooms).[20] To emphasize further the functional discreteness of the two composition elements, Utzon provided the Opera House with a massive and imposing base, then placed light graceful shells on top separated by glass walls. The granite cladding of the base thus underlined its relationship to the earth, whilst the white glazed shells drew attention to their identity as freestanding sculpture.

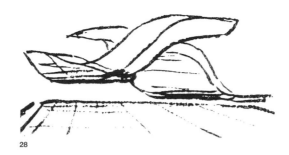

27

28

Opera Houses have traditionally been located in the central areas of cities. This simplified their design as the clumsy boot-like shape of the high fly tower over the stage area could be pushed to the back out of sight. On an exposed narrow peninsula, however, this was not a real option; on Bennelong Point, there could be no back elevation to conceal an ugly fly tower. The most favoured solution among the competition schemes was to place the two halls in line facing each other and separated by a common back stage. This entailed placing the foyers at each end, or, in one circular version, on the east and west sides. Reversing this, sharing the foyers with the auditoria facing away in opposite directions and the stage areas at the ends, would have unduly isolated the Opera House from the harbour and the city. These conventional responses ignored the site, whereas Utzon tried a completely different method by subordinating the conventional theatre arrangement to the demands of the setting. The halls are placed side by side, using to the utmost the available 102m width of the peninsula, and even extending it with a wide broadwalk to ensure continuous pedestrian access to the harbour.

Utzon's scheme was accompanied by freehand sketches of the outside elevation of the podium edge. Placing the halls on a base had the advantage of eliminating fire stairs. The podium terrain followed the section of the auditorium seating, and the halls opened directly onto the podium exposing patrons to the harbour. The auditorium-shells nestled inside the roof-shells separated by an interval. Utzon's sketches of the shell vaults touching the podium lightly and floating in space, depicted the neighbouring auditorium seating terrace levels extending out to the very edge of the podium.

A shaky start
In 1959 the future of the Sydney Opera House hung in the balance. Work on the site started on 2 March 1959, barely three weeks before a state election. The Cahill government survived, but only just with a slim majority of five seats. This was a shaky beginning, and the Coalition opposition went on the attack. Because of criticism that the Opera House project might be illegal and accusations that Cahill was deliberately withholding details of the project and its cost, an Act was drawn up in the middle of a debate about the construction of the shells. Cahill died a month later on 22 October 1959 and was succeeded by R J Heffron as Premier. Heffron presented The Sydney Opera House Act to parliament giving the Minister for Public Works legal authority and responsibility for the project. This Act authorized expenditure of up to $9.76 million (£4.88 million).

Meanwhile, Utzon was making progress. In March 1958 he submitted the new *Red Book* scheme with halls of 2,800 and 1,200 seats; an experimental theatre to seat 400; and in place of two separate meeting rooms, a room for chamber music to seat 300.

The platform – a reminder of the earth
The base consisted of three terraces in tiers, one for the hall foyers, another for the restaurant, and one at the half-level, linked by staircases across the full width. Utzon wanted to make an architectural unity out of the entire peninsula. This was the main function of the podium. Indeed, 'terrace' means a pile of earth flattened into a viewing platform; its horizontality drives the eye out into the landscape. In eighteenth-century Europe, for example, terraces overlooked the garden, acting as places with a view of nature.

27 Sketch of Japanese house by Utzon, showing the roof and platform.
28 An early conceptual sketch of the Opera House shows the building as a curved structure floating above a platform, evoking the Japanese house.
29 Jørn Utzon (right) in conversation, September 1960.
30 Utzon and Professor Ashworth (left and second from left) at Utzon's Hellebaek studio with study model of the Major Hall.

13

29

30

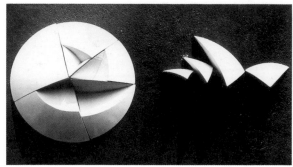

31

14

31 Model demonstrating the spherical derivation of the roof vaults, October 1961.
32 Final spherical scheme, 1962–3. Great circle rib profile in precast reinforced concrete, partially in-situ. Model of the underside vault.
33 Model of the triangular faceted ceiling of the Major Hall, at Utzon's Hellebaek studio, mid-1961.

32

33

Utzon explained the division of the Sydney Opera House into a platform and roof shells in a series of sketches of Chinese temples and Japanese houses.[21] Their roofs float above platforms, which are the same in plan but larger, as if by magic. The simple opposition of weightless shells above a massive earthbound podium makes one think of the creative interplay of Ying and Yang. His fascination with platforms originally began after a visit to Mexico to the temples of Uxmal and Chichen-Itza. There, the temple liberated the Mayans from the enclosing jungle and exposed them to the sky.[22] Utzon's use of the terrace is moreover inspired by Chinese architectural symbolism in which the earth is square and the sky is round. The rectangular base and spherical geometry of the Opera House roof vaults offers a parallel.

Besides its value as an architectural device, Utzon considered that the terrace provided a good answer to the separation of the pedestrian from motor vehicles: 'In the Sydney Opera House scheme, the idea was to let the platform cut through like a knife and separate primary and secondary functions completely. On top of the platform the spectators receive the completed work of art and beneath the platform every preparation for it takes place.'[23] Indeed, the interplay between roof and platform is axiomatic.

Less obvious, however, is the importance attached to the terrace and the sculptural interpretation of the platform as a series of related horizontal sculptural planes. Aalto did something similar in the mid-1930s in the sunken reading area of the Viipuri Library which was linked to the upper main level by a broad double stair.

The massive sculptural base of the Opera House platform expresses strength, and is also a reminder of Bennelong Point beneath it. The concourse applied Utzon's idea of a separation of pedestrians and vehicles. This required prestressed concrete beams with spans up to 49.4m. The perfectly flat paving of precast pink granite aggregate panels is laid on top and supported at every 1.83m on the beams, with a gap to allow water to drain away underneath. This avoided any need for falls and exposed drains. The beams supporting the concourse are a major structural *tour de force*. Their profile varied from a T-shape where the compression is greatest at the top, to a U-section trough where the maximum compression is at the bottom. The resulting twisted surfaces intersect in sine curves.

The monolithic character of the podium was increased by covering it with similar precast paving panels in a simple vertical pattern. The wall panels were 1.22m (4ft) wide and varied in length up to a maximum of 9.1m (30ft). They had a T-T cross-section consisting of a 7.62cm (3in) thick concrete slab with a finished face of exposed granite chip strengthened at the back by two 28cm (11in) deep concrete ribs. These wall panels splay out at an angle in places to form hoods over the door and window openings.

The roof vaults – a reminder of the sky
The clouds from the terrace of Kronborg Castle in Utzon's sketches hover above the horizon or assume more architectonic interlocking curved forms that are truly Baroque in their appearance. Finding a geometry for the shells was the most difficult task Utzon faced on winning the competition. The structural engineering firm of Ove Arup and Partners, who had been appointed in the middle of 1957, advised Cahill against making an early start but political expediency prevailed. The engineers could not design the base without first establishing the roof loads it would carry. The roof surfaces at the beginning lacked a defined geometry. The competition scheme showed four main pairs of curved surfaces for each hall. These geometrically undefined surfaces were connected to each other by a further series of side surfaces. The scale was very large.

In mid-1961, Utzon telephoned Ove Arup from Copenhagen to say he had the solution to the roof geometry.[24] It was deceptively simple: the roof would consist of spherical planes from the same common sphere. The competition roof surfaces had been free sculptural shapes, whilst the final shapes were part of a large sphere. The Major Hall roof surface derived from a sphere of 75m radius. Arups had explored over eight geometries in four years starting with parabolic surfaces, moving to ellipsoid schemes and then on to circular arc rib proposals.[25]

Contrary to popular belief, the inspiration for this spherical geometry came from a segmented orange – not from white sails.[26] The choice of a spherical surface achieved several things: it established a geometry of great clarity; the convexity of the surface pushes outwards and upwards, and so makes us more aware of the universe. The roofs are a source of radiation – a fundamentally

34

35

Baroque technique to the extent that the individual roof vaults are fractions of a pre-existent whole, and their very incompleteness makes them appear to dissolve in infinity. White tiles were chosen as a covering to serve light; their appearance is never static but varies according to the light conditions. The Opera House always looks different depending on where you stand. Its images embrace us, and this serves to engender a feeling of macrocosm – a very Baroque feeling indeed.

Each main vault was constructed by gluing together large (typically 4.6m long x 10,160kg) precast rib segments with a two-part epoxy – an innovation at the time. The ribs radiate from the podium and become wider up the vault. The cross section of each rib varies from a T at the pedestal to a solid and then an open Y at its uppermost. The ribs radiate from a solid concrete pedestal at springing to a ridge beam, while the rib segments are held together like a necklace by prestressing tendons made up of 15.2mm diameter strands.

Utzon clad the external vault surface with two types of off-white tiles – one glazed, one matt. These tiles were fixed to 44.5mm thick precast concrete chevron-shaped tile lids 2.3m long, which express the roof-ribs underneath. The tiles resemble great fish scales glistening in the sunlight.

Glass waterfalls – the glass walls
Hanging glass curtain walls fill the open ends and the sides of the concrete rib-vaults of the Opera House. Utzon sought to manage the transition from the vertical vaults, and the horizontal podium at the northern ends over the lounge terraces happen in a very organic way. To visualize his intention we might imagine a soap film stretched between the vault ribs and the podium edge. Utzon even constructed a simple model in his office using cotton string with vertical and horizontal strings stretched across the vault ends in a minimal surface.[27] This basic saddle-surface simulated the curvature he sought. The vertical section is not unlike Kenzo Tange's Yoyogi Swimming Stadium for the 1964 Tokyo Olympics. Utzon wanted the walls to be expressed as a hanging curtain, a kind of glass waterfall that swings out as it descends to form a canopy over the lounge terraces and foyer entrances. Indeed, the north terraces are really great verandas with a glass canopy cover overlooking the harbour.

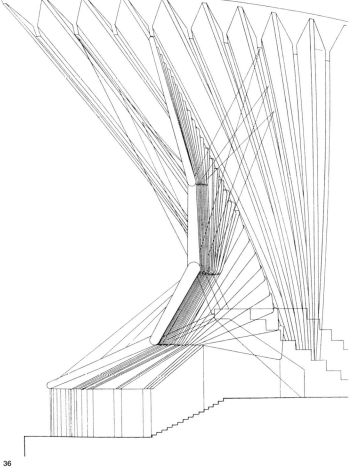

36

34 In-situ concrete ribbed vault pedestal and glass wall at south foyer of the Opera Theatre.
35 Glass wall of the Opera Theatre's south foyer.
36 Major Hall, section through northern glass walls, c1961.

37

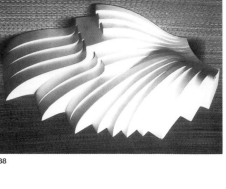

38

37 Model of west elevation showing spherical scheme, in-situ and precast reinforced concrete, 1962.

38 Plaster model of Minor Hall showing half auditorium shell radial segments with concave profile – the final development of the 'stepped cloud' scheme, February, 1962.

39 System drawings for stepped cylindrical surfaces in the acoustical reflectors of the Minor Hall.

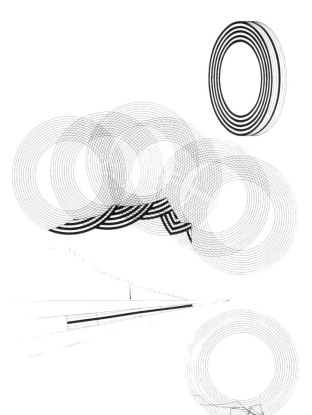

The mullions were to be built up of plywood with a hot-bonded skin of bronze on the exterior, spaced 91cm (3ft), with the glass sheets attached in overlapping positions. Each was built up of 60cm (2ft) wide plywood elements made up of 12.7mm seven-ply Soraya.[28] The drawings showed a series of stepped mullions fanning out in section like a time exposure photograph of a bird's wing in flight.

Utzon was justifiably enthusiastic about plywood which for its weight is a very strong material – an important detail since the glass walls were suspended from the vaults. In the early sixties Ralph Symonds was the only company in the world with the capacity to manufacture plywood in lengths of up to 15m. The company later supplied aluminium clad plywood panels on the exterior of the Australian National Maritime Museum at Darling Harbour, and panels throughout the New Australian Parliament House. Davis Hughes' refusal to approve the plywood mock-ups for the auditoria ceilings was a major cause – though not the only one – which precipitated the crisis of 28 February 1966. As it turned out, plywood was used for the moulded wall and ceiling panels and the shaped seat shells in the halls.

Mother cylinder – the halls

Fitting the auditoria under the roof vaults proved difficult. The acoustical requirements for large halls was poorly understood and acoustical model research was still in its infancy in the early sixties. The ceiling of the Philharmonic Hall of the Lincoln Centre in New York, for example, was rebuilt three times at a cost of over $2 million.[29] The belief that a dual-use auditorium could deliver good acoustics was not challenged. A reduction in the number of seats from 3,500 to 2,800 brought it nearer to the maximum size for a dual-use hall suited to concerts and opera. The seating arrangement with 1,800 in the auditorium proper, and 1,000 on the stage behind the orchestra for concerts followed the precedent of the San Francisco War Memorial Opera House. At concerts a large temporary sound-reflecting ceiling sealed off the stage loft and was later removed for opera performances.

Utzon conceived the halls with plywood ceilings consisting of giant, freely undulating folded beams.[30] These structural beams, spanning from the proscenium arch to the rear balcony, followed exactly the acoustic profile for the halls. Most concert halls had panels attached beneath a supporting structure. In the Sydney Opera House, however, the auditoria shells were themselves structural being self-supporting and partly suspended from the concrete roof vaults. Utzon, therefore, undertook the difficult task of harmonizing the acoustical shape and volumetric demands with the structural.

An aspect often overlooked in the building is the relationship of the auditoria to the roof vaults. Utzon sought to insert an inter-space between the two; in this way, the patron could look up and follow the line of the concrete ribs over the auditorium shell. Utzon compared this with a walnut shell and its kernel; the kernel is different in character to the hard outer shell yet in harmony with it. Today, the Concert Hall pushes against the ribs and looks anything but graceful as the separation space was reduced to a minimum in order to cram as many seats as possible into the Concert Hall.

Utzon designed numerous schemes for the halls in his quest for perfection: the first, illustrated in the 1958 *Red Book* and referred to as the 'stepped cloud' scheme, consisted of a low narrow hall stepped like a fan across the hall with vertical side walls; this was succeeded by more elaborate concave shaped interiors and sloping side walls to fit under the roof in 1960. Utzon persisted with concave geometries until the appointment of the Berlin acoustic consultants Professors Lothar Cremer and Werner Gabler in August 1962, when, at their suggestion, he began studies involving convex ceiling profiles. In August 1960, he had begun to develop a prismatic triangular faceted shell for the Major Hall and this, though later abandoned, yielded very encouraging results acoustically. In December 1962 Utzon made an important breakthrough in the Minor Hall[31] which led him to abandon the triangular faceted scheme for the Major Hall and apply a similar system and geometry to it as well. This proved much more difficult, the acoustic problems being compounded by the dual-use requirement and changes in the seating. More than a year after the *Yellow Book* submission (January 1962), Utzon was instructed to relocate most of the seats in front of the orchestra in the

40

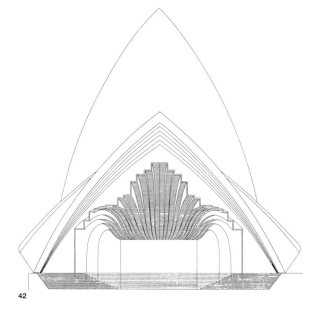

41

Major Hall. By 18 November 1963, he had a solution. This involved adding a balcony to the back and sides to provide 2,000 seats for opera and 2,500 for concerts in the auditorium proper. Professor Cremer was the principal acoustical consultant for the Berlin Philharmonie where his introduction of the 'vineyard-mountain-system' of terraces and intermediate walls to step the auditorium floor had proved a considerable success. Similar vineyard terraces were introduced into the Major Hall in early 1964.[32] Rapid progress was made in its design in 1964 aided by the presence in Sydney of Cremer's assistant Nutsch. By early 1965, within days of his removal from the project, Utzon had arrived at a workable solution to the Major Hall which resulted in the production of ¼ in scale drawings illustrating a similar system and geometry to the Minor Hall comprised of radial plywood wedges supporting a series of convex acoustic profiles.[33]

What is one to make of all this? Utzon wanted the halls to be based on a strong generating idea, and to be integrated down to the smallest element in order that each element reflected the whole thing; in essence, he wanted a kit of standard parts assembled in a flexible manner. This did not allow him to proceed in a piecemeal way which is what actually happened later; every aspect of the problem had to relate to every other aspect in a disciplined manner so that it was in harmony, each part with each other. The spherical solution of the roof geometry already proved the value of this approach.

The third and final phase schemes were based on radial arcs generated by a rolling cylinder.[34] The hall schemes shown in the 1962 *Yellow Book* were done before the idea of the cylinder emerged. The Minor Hall is shown with a curved ceiling of radial pieces with vertical side walls that curve over and rise in steps at the highest point

under the vault ridge; it sweeps down towards the proscenium opening. During the third phase a cylindrical scheme was adopted for the Minor Hall and applied to the Major Hall in a rhythmical sequence of convex radial wedges. In the *Yellow Book*, the Major Hall has a multi-faceted folded plate vault made up of triangular plates that rest on slender elongated triangular shaped buttresses which are left open at the back for egress. This folded plate design was entirely different from that of the Minor Hall; while the new final phase designs for both halls are as similar as brother and sister.

The auditoria ceiling profiles were generated by a standard cylinder that moves forward in a wave-like motion, which suggested a powerful metaphor for the ceilings since sound is a wave propagated in an elastic medium such as air or water. Utzon later expanded the idea to encompass the undersea world of the coral reef. In a last detailed model left behind in Australia, the underside of the slim radial wedges of the Opera Theatre ceiling were painted in alternating white and muted coral stripes with vertical faces in gold. This extremely sumptuous effect is not unlike Japanese Noh and Kabuki theatre which Utzon admired; furthermore, it can be seen as richly Baroque in its elaboration of cylindrical ceiling elements converging on the opera stage in a rainbow of coral-reef colours. It provides a surprising and fittingly dramatic conclusion to the processional sequence from the outside ending in the theatre.

Fitting more seats into the Major Hall entailed mounting a false timber floor on the existing concrete slab. This was poured long before the programme changes; once this was done new stairs were inevitable. A great virtue of the original scheme was that the two auditoria accessed directly onto the podium, thus eliminating the need for stairs. The additional stairs, however, take up valuable space and thwart the relationship with the podium edge.

With Utzon's departure and the arrival of a new team, led by Peter Hall, who replaced Utzon in mid 1967, major changes were made to the programme for the theatres. Without warning opera was eliminated from the Major Hall which was renamed the Concert Hall. The removal of the dual-purpose acoustic requirement simplified matters considerably; $3.84 million worth of stage machinery, which was to have gone into the understage space, became redundant and was never used.

40 Concert Hall from the southern stage area looking towards the auditorium. This illustrates the changes made to Utzon's original scheme of a raised ceiling profile and vineyard terraces.
41 Concert Hall, lower seating terrace from the west side of the auditorium.
42 Cross section of Minor Hall (Opera Theatre) auditorium towards the stage, drawing from the *Yellow Book*.

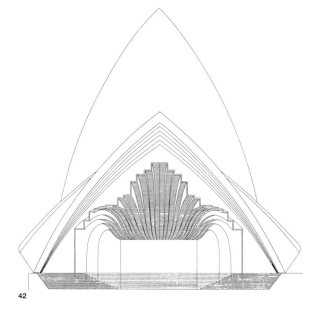

42

43

18

43 Model of the Major Hall (Concert Hall), 1965.
44 Architecture students demonstrating for Utzon's reinstatement as architect of the Opera House; the Opera House stands in construction in the background.
45 Minor Hall (Opera Theatre) roof: erection of rib segments using three tower cranes and a specially designed erection arch (seen in the foreground).

46, 47 Eastern corridor of the Concert Hall looking towards the northern bar area opposite the harbour (46) and down the stairs from north bar area end (47).
48 Minor Hall ceiling, cross sectional elevation of back of auditorium, showing plywood tube rib system, November 1965.
49 Minor Hall, plan and elevation of radial shell segments, July 1964.

Square arches – the corridors

Utzon needed to line the corridor circulation spaces between the rehearsal rooms and dressing rooms to hide the building services on the ceilings and walls – an almost impossible task for the designer. To hide such things as ventilation ducts, electricity, water, fire protection, etc, while at the same time leaving them accessible for inspection and maintenance, Utzon introduced a system of panel units consisting of a moulded plywood panel 40cm (16in) wide and approximately 12.7cm (5in) deep, and a plywood slat. When assembled they formed an arch that lent in or out like an arm bent at the elbow. The corridor solution, like the glass wall mullions and the plywood beams for the auditoria shells, was part of the same idea of a flexible kit of plywood components.

The inspiration came from a remarkable row of *torii* on the approach to the Inari Shrine in Kyoto. At the Inari Shrine, closely spaced posts are spanned by beams to form a tunnel around the meandering stone-paved pathway. Light breaks through at the sides. Here, as elsewhere, Utzon was guided by the principle of harnessing a few standard components to produce a more varied and human environment. These curved plywood wall panels sat on a rail at floor level and covered otherwise exposed services on the wall. They were connected at the top by pivots to large plywood slats under any ducts to the opposite wall, and the services above the slats were hidden by high-intensity lighting and by painting the ceiling a dark colour. The approach was adopted by Peter Hall with one important change: similar panels were used for the walls and ceilings, the ceiling slats being dropped entirely and a strictly rectangular geometry was followed to maximize the corridor space.

Not by chance – Jørn Utzon's removal

On 1 May 1965, a Liberal-Country Party Coalition government led by Robert Askin won office after 24 years of Labor rule and pledged to do something about the escalating costs and delays in the completion of the Opera House. Premier Askin immediately appointed Davis Hughes as his Minister for Public Works. Hughes had campaigned hard on the issue of more roads and dams in country areas, and he wished to be seen doing something. The Liberal Party lout and the Country Party opportunist were therefore well matched since Askin had long been a leading critic of Utzon.

Hughes first ascertained what stand the Royal Australian Institute of Architects would take, and whether it would support Utzon.[35] He must have been surprised and delighted to find a willing supporter in R A Gilling, the New South Wales Chapter President. In October, he took the next step to freeze Utzon out by removing the authority for the payment of fees from the Opera House executive committee and stopping regular payments. Starved of money, with outstanding fees unpaid and unable to pay his own staff, and with no cooperation forthcoming from his client, Utzon handed a letter to the Minister on 28 February 1966, temporarily withdrawing his services. Hughes then pounced.[36] The media were instantly informed that Utzon had resigned. In fact, it resembled an execution more than a resignation – a resignation it was not; and, indeed, Utzon's exact words were: '… you have forced me to leave the job'.[37]

At the height of the crisis 'The Sydney Opera House Affair' divided Sydney.[38] Hughes' chief worry was that he might not be able to find architects to finish the Opera House. His concerns proved groundless although his removal of Utzon did provoke a mutiny among architects within his own department. Senior architects opposed the Minister and refused to sign a prepared statement supporting his action.

After Utzon had gone, Peter Hall was installed with nearly identical powers to Utzon – little had changed except the name of the architect. Work stopped and expenditure continued to rise even further.

The real motives behind Utzon's removal were political. Hughes was an instrument of rural revenge – the project had been a Labor Party idea and it had to be purged of this taint. Sacking the Opera House executive committee was far too dangerous. Utzon was the obvious fall guy; and as a foreigner he was an easy target.

44

45

46

47

Moreover, private architects in Sydney depended on the Public Works Department for work so they could be relied on not to cause difficulties.

During the Opera House debate in Parliament later that year the previous Minister for Public Works, Mr Ryan, summed up Davis Hughes' tactics: 'The withdrawal of Utzon from the Opera House was not by chance or accident but the result of a campaign deliberately embarked upon by the Minister … I suggest to the House that it occurred for a political reason, and in the process the consultant [Ove Arup & Partners] and the Institute of Architects were brought in to bolster the case…'[39]

The amount – $18 million – spent while Utzon was in charge was less than one quarter of what Hughes would later spend, and it amounted to a trifling 17.6% of the final cost. Hughes represented country people and farmers who knew little, and cared even less, about what happened to the Opera House, but they deeply resented any money spent on cultural pursuits in far-away Sydney. If the Askin government is remembered at all today, it is not for completing the Sydney Opera House, but for a record of corruption and involvement in major vice trades, illegal casinos and SP Bookmaking, unparalleled in the state's history.[40] The Utzon crisis conveniently diverted public attention from the corrupt practices of the Askin government.

Indeed, Utzon had seen at their first meeting in 1965 what the new Minister for Public Works intended: '… he had decided to take over and become the man most closely associated with the Opera House'.[41] Davis Hughes hungered for attention and the political spotlight as the person most closely identified with the Opera House. And this meant getting rid of Utzon.

Change of programme –1966–9

On 19 April 1966, Hughes announced the new consortium assigned to complete the Opera House: it consisted of Peter Hall, then aged 34, a young designer from the Government Architect's staff who had previously supported Utzon, and who subsequently changed his mind; Lionel Todd, aged 36, from the firm of Hanson, Todd and Partners; and David Littlemore, aged 55, of Rudder, Littlemore, Rudder. Hall was responsible for design. The fourth member, E H Farmer, the Government architect, gave advice and oversaw the project in his role as client. Shortly afterwards, Utzon left Sydney secretly with his family to avoid the media circus.

The Opera House was now ready for work to start on the interiors. Stage I, including the steps, concourse, platforms and seating tiers had finished in January 1963; by January 1967 the last tile lid was lowered into position and the roof vaults were complete. After that nothing happened.

The new architects were faced with two questions: what to do about the seating capacity and acoustics. The Opera House brief had called for a Major Hall with a proscenium type theatre for dual-use for both concerts and opera, with the emphasis on concerts. The requirement for opera entailed a tower above the stage and seven elevators for access below the stage for props, scenery and other equipment. This caused a spectacular public brawl between the Australian Broadcasting Commission, demanding the Major Hall for concerts, and the Elizabethan Theatre Trust, demanding joint use for opera. Now, in the 1990s, the ABC no longer requires use of the Sydney Opera House as it once did: the Town Hall has been refurbished; other major halls have been built in western Sydney; and the Sydney Symphony Orchestra goes on tour and has a rehearsal hall and home in the new ABC Centre at Ultimo, Sydney.

Orchestral concerts require halls with a large volume and a short reverberation time; while opera requires the audience to be close to a large stage, with better sight lines, considerable wing space and machinery for scene changing, and a proscenium arch which traps part of the performance. The relationship of the orchestra is also different for opera.

On 7 June 1966, the General Manager of the ABC wrote to the New South Wales Government Architect to push the ABC's demands for a hall with a seating capacity of not less than 2,800, stage space for a large choir and orchestra, and acoustics with a reverberation time in the middle frequency range of 2.0 seconds.[42] The minister asked Hall, Todd and Littlemore to investigate, and Peter Hall set off on a three-month world study tour to research the design of dual-purpose auditoria.

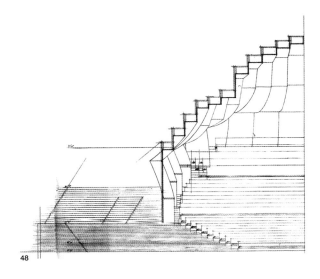

48

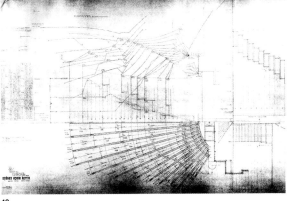

49

50

51

50, 51 Ground floor, Opera Theatre under stage area looking south towards the transport stage platforms.
52 Ground plan of the Opera House with both Halls – the larger has 3,500 seats, the smaller 1,200 – competition scheme, 1956.
53 Longitudinal section through Major Hall with timber ceiling.
54 Plan of Major Hall.

In January 1967 Peter Hall's report, *First Review of Programme*, recommended the Major Hall be made a concert hall to meet the ABC's criteria and rejected its use as a multi-purpose hall. He suggested increasing both the volume and seating, removal of the stage tower, and allowing the ceiling to sweep uninterrupted from one end of the hall to the other. The Cabinet adopted the Review's recommendations and, on 21 March, Hughes announced that there would be no opera in the Major Hall which was to become a single-purpose concert hall. This shifted the responsibility for opera to the Minor Hall which was found to be too small. The Minor Hall, as the Opera Theatre, would have to seat 1,500 instead of 1,100, and the orchestra pit would need to be enlarged to accommodate around 80 musicians. It was a radical rethink.

There were other changes: the Drama Theatre in the podium which was to have been a proscenium theatre seating around 500 was increased to 700–750 persons, and would become an experimental theatre; the area directly below the Major Hall's stage would be converted to a large rehearsal/recording studio; and the set-changing area next to this would become a fourth auditorium.

A year and a half later, the government approved the new programme and work on Stage III commenced in early 1969. 49 months – four years – had been lost. In 1968 the budget was increased from $50 million to $85 million.

Completing the interiors – Stage III
To this day the experience of acoustic sound remains beyond the skill of scientists to measure and quantify. Whereas the shoe-box shape represented the ideal in the fifties and sixties, it is now rejected because its sound is too 'frontal'.[43] These days, halls shaped like Utzon's designs are *de rigueur*. It was not recognized until the late sixties that because of binaural hearing, sound quality depends more on an enveloping 'closeness', and this is assisted by strong lateral sound reflections.[44]

The revised design of the Major Hall was based on outmoded acoustic theory that has since been repudiated. It was thought that reverberation time was a reliable indicator of musical quality because it could be measured. Sound quality is not accessible to modelling and to testing. Reverberation time is largely a factor of volume; to increase it, the volume must be increased. A reverberation time of

2.2 seconds remains an optimum goal – extremely difficult to achieve in a hall for 3,000. (Successful nineteenth-century halls were half that size.) The ABC's demand for no less than 3,000 seats was based on purely commercial calculations, and mitigated against a good acoustics outcome.

The Concert Hall
For his tests of the Concert Hall and the Opera Theatre, acoustician V L Jordan used 1:10 scale models made from thick plywood varnished on the inside. Seats were made of continuous strips of neoprene with individual blocks topped by squares of cardboard to simulate people. A high-tension spark source which radiated sound pulses of extremely short duration was employed to measure the 'early decay time' (EDT). Jordan compared the average value of EDT in the audience area to the value in the stage area to obtain a coefficient he called the 'inversion index'. He required the index never to be less than 1.0: to comply, the EDT should be higher in the audience area than in the stage area.[45] It was later found that the inversion index was improved by suspending convex plexiglass reflectors above the orchestra stage. In general, the values of EDT for the orchestra level seating were deficient. A way to improve this was to reduce the dominance of ceiling reflections; this meant moving the ceiling further up and straightening it, at the same time bringing the side walls in and recessing the side boxes into the walls. The effect of this was a return to the long shoe-box shape of the first design, the main difference being that now the stage was no longer at one end, but nearer to the centre.

A reverberation time of 2.2 seconds required approximately 9.3 cub m per seat. In the case of the Concert Hall, this suggested a volume of 25,107 cub m.

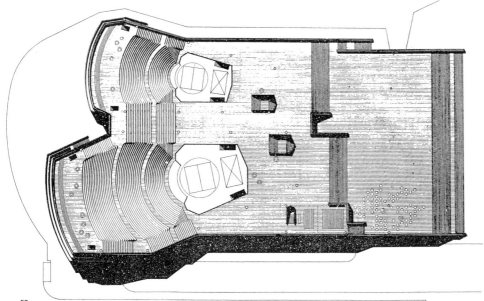

52

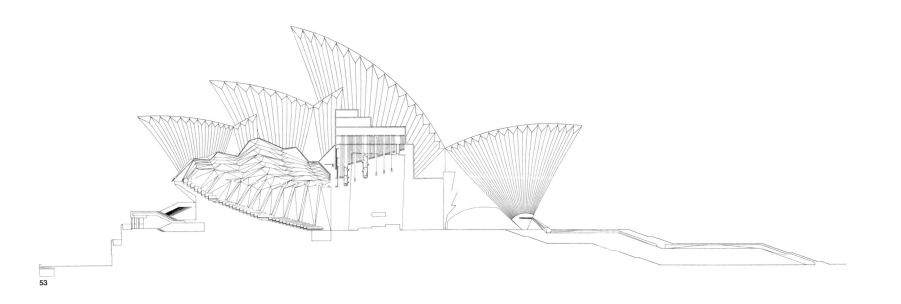

53

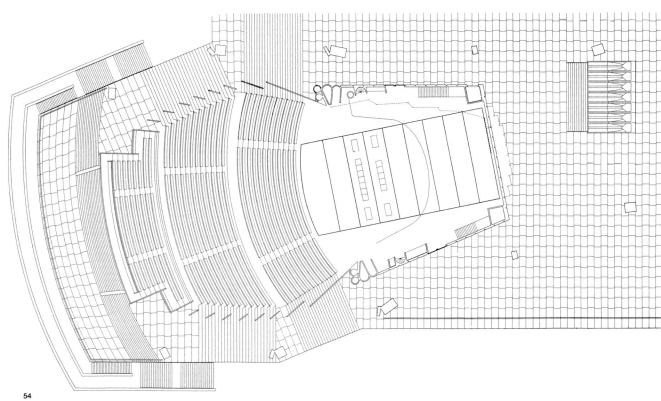

54

55

56

22

55 Concert Hall, eastern
side boxes.
56 Northern lounge and bar
area of Concert Hall.
57 Concert Hall, suspended
plexiglass sound reflectors or
'clouds' above the orchestra
area correct EDT deficiency.
58 Hans Scharoun,
Philarmonie, Berlin, 1956–63,
east–west section.

57

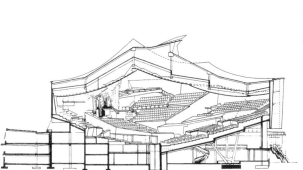

58

The actual volume is less – 24,069 cub m –
giving a reverberation time of 2.1 seconds
or slightly under. The hall has 2,690 seats –
short of the 3,000 demanded by the ABC
and less than the 2,800 provided by Utzon.

Even to achieve that amount meant
enlarging the seating area by building out
over the side foyers with cantilevered
galleries, and introducing a very large
cantilever at the north end of the building
to create the terrace seating.[46] This
effectively destroyed the relationship of
the halls and the roof vaults; and it is
especially disappointing to find the side
foyers cluttered with stairs and signs that
detract from the noble quality of the
promenade.

Peter Hall was at first influenced by
Utzon, although the final double-spade
shape is really indebted to Hans
Scharoun's Berlin Philharmonie Concert
Hall (1956–63) with the position of the
orchestra stage now moved towards the
centre. The Berlin Philharmonie seats
2,200 – 369 less than the Concert Hall.
Peter Hall was less successful than
Scharoun however in focusing the
audience on the orchestra, and the result
is not so much music at the centre, as
an audience removed to the back and
squashed up against the sides. The ceiling
is vaguely reminiscent of Utzon, with radial
beam-like segments that step out from the
walls to form side boxes which meet in a
crown piece above the stage. This had to
be lifted to decrease the dominance of
ceiling reflections. Furthermore, the
introduction of the crown piece to
emphasize the orchestra was a blunder.
Its height is such that it is only remotely
connected to the orchestra and quite
unrelated to the overall radial theme of
the ceiling.

The problem of excluding outside noise,
especially from the large halls, was a
constant worry. The completed ceilings
were therefore constructed with an outer
'cocoon' of sprayed concrete separated
from an inner layer of 12mm plywood on a
backing of 25mm plasterboard by a void
housing the services. This acoustic shell is
supported from the vaults by steel trusses
hung between the precast concrete ribs.
A plasterboard backing was added to
retain the base and thereby increase the
warmth of the hall.

The Opera Theatre

The Opera Theatre was less critical. As
completed, it has 1,547 seats in stalls,
dress circle and side boxes or loges. The
volume is about a third of the Concert Hall.
The maximum length is 34.44m – half the
67m of the Concert Hall – but it is only
slightly (7.62m) narrower. And the Opera
Theatre is better proportioned. To satisfy
his inversion index requirement, Jordan
moved the ceiling of the Opera Theatre
upwards; each time he did this there was
an improvement. In the final model the
ceiling was raised to the maximum
permitted by the concrete rib-vaults.
Even so, suspended reflectors were
required above the orchestra seating area.

The interior of the Opera Theatre is
subordinated to the stage. The walls are
black and the ceiling has an interesting
faceted shape. The elegant purpose-
designed seats of white birch with red
wool (originally in hide and changed in
1994) and the off-form concrete of the
gallery fronts is impressive. Artist John
Coburn's stage curtains are especially
arresting, with their heroic scale and vivid
colours, even more so when the house
lights are up.

The aesthetic of these interiors is one
of great restraint, supported by a limited
palette of materials and correspondingly
minimal application of colour. The slotted
and moulded birch panels which cover the
services on the walls perform the same
function on the ceilings.

**Cones and cylinders –
rethinking the glass walls**

Peter Hall rejected the glass wall scheme
left by Utzon. It was replaced by a very
different scheme which sought to produce
a smooth transparent glass curtain. Utzon
had intended to use plywood mullion
elements, but this was vetoed by Minister

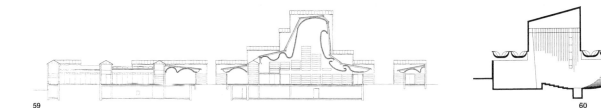

59

60

Davis Hughes, and it was replaced by steel. The walls follow a roughly similar profile swinging out in front of the vaults as they descend in two stages to form a roughly saddle-like surface. The glass below the canopy tilts inwards to oppose the upper glass canopy. The same outward tilt is mimicked by the side glass walls which incline back in towards the ribs above door height. The two planes meet tangentially over a bronze extrusion.

Work on the glass walls began in 1970 and was completed two years later. A laminate was selected consisting of a layer of clear plate or float glass in two thicknesses, and a 6mm layer of 'demitopaze' tinted glass, with a 0.76mm thick interlayer of clear polyvinyl butyral.[47] The standard thickness is 18.8mm, with 20.8mm laminate in areas requiring greater strength. Each glass sheet is supported along its vertical sides by extruded manganese bronze T-section glazing bars with a cover piece screwed on afterwards. The glazing bars are attached to supporting steel mullions by an adjustable fixing bracket at approximately 0.9m centres. The mullions consist of two parallel 90mm diameter tubes 530mm apart, joined by a 6mm plate web.

Hall designed the end glass walls for maximum transparency and the steel was painted a pinkish-brown to match the colour of oxidized steel. The north glass wall of the Concert Hall looks very clumsy seen from most directions. Two large dog ears poke out over the corners of the north lounges. Since the glass could not be warped or curved, it was cut to create a simple curved surface based on a combination of cones and cylinders. Starting from the roof rib, the surface is a vertical elliptical cylinder and becomes the upper part of a cone, then has a lower cone base to connect it to the edge of the podium.

Completing Utzon's vision – the Wran improvements

In 1976 Labor was back in government, led by Neville Wran, a former barrister, who had once offered to advise Utzon during the Opera House crisis. When it opened on 20 October 1973, the Sydney Opera House was still far from complete. In his haste, Hughes built a hideous cheap-looking covered metal walkway that hid the Opera House; there was no car park for patrons; and the forecourt was paved in bitumen.

Under Neville Wran's government, the Special Projects section of the Department of Public Works, led by Andrew Andersons, redeveloped the entire Circular Quay precinct at a cost of $62 million in time for the 1988 Bicentennial celebrations. This included the reconstruction of the Circular Quay East broadwalk in accordance with sketch proposals left by Utzon. The broadwalk was extended around the Circular Quay foreshore to the bridge. The Circular Quay East forecourt is on two levels, with restaurants and shops in the covered walkway on the lower level leading under the main Opera House concourse. A 300m long glass roof was added connecting the forecourt to the revamped Circular Quay Railway Station. This laminated glass and steel walkway has a minimum number of columns to maximize its transparency. Emerging at the northern end of the Circular Quay East walkway, the Opera House forecourt, which is now paved in granite sets with a smooth border, sweeps around in a lazy curve that progressively introduces the Opera House. The upper forecourt has also been pulled back to reveal the activities in the forecourt terrace below it.

Picking up the pieces – Utzon's reputation

The Opera House crisis devastated Utzon. The project had meant so much to him. Furthermore, the press failed in its job – it never seriously investigated Davis Hughes' claims about Utzon, nor did it check the so-called facts. Had it done so, a very different story would have emerged.

Today, Utzon's position as one of the most original and important designers of the twentieth century is assured.[48] He broke out of the functionalist straitjacket to show that buildings could be romantic and expressive; and he rethought the industrial prefabrication of standard elements to produce complex forms that depart from the strict rectangular order of Mies van der Rohe and his generation. The Kuwait National Assembly (1979–81), for example, is a huge wonderful concrete tent, several times larger than the Sydney Opera House. While he was working on the Opera House, Utzon entered the competition for the Essen Opera House, and won third place after Aalto and Hans Scharoun. Utzon's design for the Municipal Theatre in Zurich, meanwhile, developed ideas taken from the Opera House: its roof was composed of beams like the ones in the concourse, while the theatre had a ceiling with a cylindrical motif similar to the last design for the Opera Theatre.

59 Utzon's Bagsvaerd Church, Copenhagen, 1976, longitudinal section.
60 Utzon's Municipal Theatre, Zurich, 1964, longitudinal section (competition project).
61 Opera Theatre, view towards the stage showing John Coburn's stage curtains.
62 The appearance of the main north glass wall of the Concert Hall is marred by ugly projecting dog ears of glass.

23

61

62

Photographs

The Sydney Opera House,
west elevation. Panoramic
view from Campbell's Cove
across Sydney Cove showing
the Bounty replica.
The Opera House is a theatre-
at-the-water's-edge looking
across the harbour-stage.

Above The Opera House was conceived as a 'house of festivals', reached by means of a processional approach leading by stages to the theatres at the end of Bennelong Point. Southern panoramic view looking towards the restaurant and Concert Hall from Circular Quay East. A covered walkway and promenade leads to the Opera House forecourt.

Right The roof shells are reminiscent of the sky, while the ribs which form each shell are covered by precast concrete lids of white, fish scale-like tiles. East facade of the Opera Theatre shells facing Farm Cove from Man of War jetty.

Left The structure and pre-stressing anchorage pockets of the roof shells are visible on looking underneath. View showing Concert Hall roof shell A1, and looking west between the southern foyer and restaurant shell, with Campbell's Cove in the background.

Above The inspiration for the spherical geometry of the roofs came from a segmented orange. Here a slice from the orange stands on its tip – east elevation of southern foyer Concert Hall shell A1 with the shadow of the Opera Theatre shell across it.

Left Hanging glass walls fill the open ends and sides of the concrete rib-vaults. East elevation of the south-facing glass wall and shell over Bennelong Restaurant.

Above The prestressed engineering of the rib-vaults produces its own highly sculptural results. Cast in-situ concrete pedestal of the A1 southernmost roof shell above the Concert Hall foyer.

Left The roof vaults were inspired by clouds over the water of Øre Sound opposite Kronborg Castle at Helsingør. The spherical geometry of the roof is apparent in this view of the east side of the Opera Theatre roof.

Right The chevron-shaped precast tile lids that encase the ribs of the roof vaults were covered with glazed white tiles in the centre and matt tiles marking the edges.

Left In-situ concrete shell pedestal and the glass wall enclosing the southern Opera Theatre foyer. The 18.8mm tinted glass laminate is supported by steel mullions fabricated from two 90mm pipes, 53cm apart, connected by a web and bolted to corbels on the underside of the concrete rib segments.

Above Underside of Bennelong Restaurant roof showing the pattern of precast rib segments which rise to meet the ridge beam at the centre.

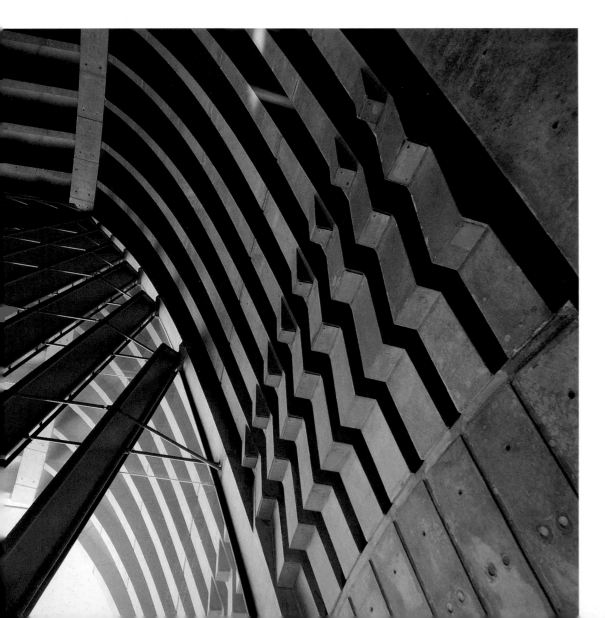

Left and above Glass wall of the southern foyer serving the Concert Hall. Detail of the steel mullions supporting the glass wall and fixing to the precast rib segments (left); detail of the infill glass walls enclosing the access corridors around the Concert Hall under the shell skirt (above, right). These repeat the same outward tilt as the glass walls but thrust inwards below door head height.

Right Underside of shell A1 over the main southern foyer adjoining the Concert Hall, is intercepted by the vertical rhythm of the prefabricated timber panelling.

Left and below Side corridors lead around the Concert Hall and into the auditorium – an essential ingredient of Utzon's concept of a processional approach sequence from the forecourt leading up to its climax in the performance space. East corridor of the Concert Hall looking north (bottom left) and south (bottom right), and east corridor viewed from the higher north end (left) looking down the space between the roof shells and the auditorium shells.

Right The northern foyer and bar area of the Concert Hall overlooking Sydney Harbour resembles a large glazed veranda with its upswept glass canopy. Patrons flood onto the lounge terrace during the intervals to enjoy the lights and movement of the harbour.

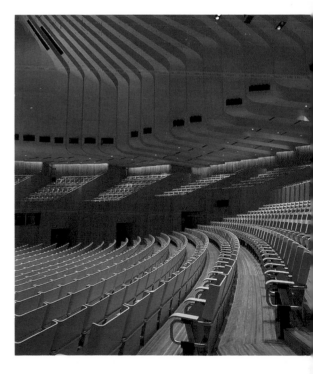

Left Interior of the Concert Hall from the north looking towards the orchestra stage and pipe organ. The focus on the orchestra has been lost. The seating arrangements of vineyard terraces is indebted to Hans Scharoun's Berlin Philharmonie Concert Hall completed in 1963.

Above and right Concert Hall view from behind the stage, looking south (above) and view looking west across the Concert Hall at the level of the first terrace (right), the second terrace seating is separated from the first by a sound reflective wall. The plywood ceiling panels rise centripetally from the seating and curve over to meet above the stage area.

Above Southern foyer of the Opera Theatre; timber panelling hides the back of the stage tower.

Right Eastern corridor leads opera goers to the Opera Theatre and side boxes which are a feature of the auditorium. The corridor rises in a series of stairs to the north in step with the rake of the theatre.

Left Opera Theatre auditorium looking east from the upper level of the front side boxes. The orchestra pit is under the stage.

Above View towards the stage of the Opera Theatre shows Australian artist John Coburn's vivid and colourful stage curtains.

Above The aesthetic of the
Opera Theatre is one of great
restraint. View across Opera
Theatre looking west; side boxes
and black walls are enlivened by
red wool seat covers in pale
birch veneer plywood shells.

Drawings

Location plan

1 Bennelong Point
2 Sydney Cove
3 Circular Quay
4 The Sydney Opera House
5 Opera House forecourt
6 1,100-space underground
   car park (1993)
7 covered walkway and
   promenade
8 Cahill Expressway
   (Circular Quay Railway
   Station)
9 Royal Botanic Gardens
10 Government House
11 Macquarie Street
   (NSW State Parliament)

0 ————— 200 metres

0 ————— 200 yards

Site plan

1 Concert Hall
2 Opera Theatre
3 main restaurant
4 concourse
5 forecourt
6 North Broadwalk

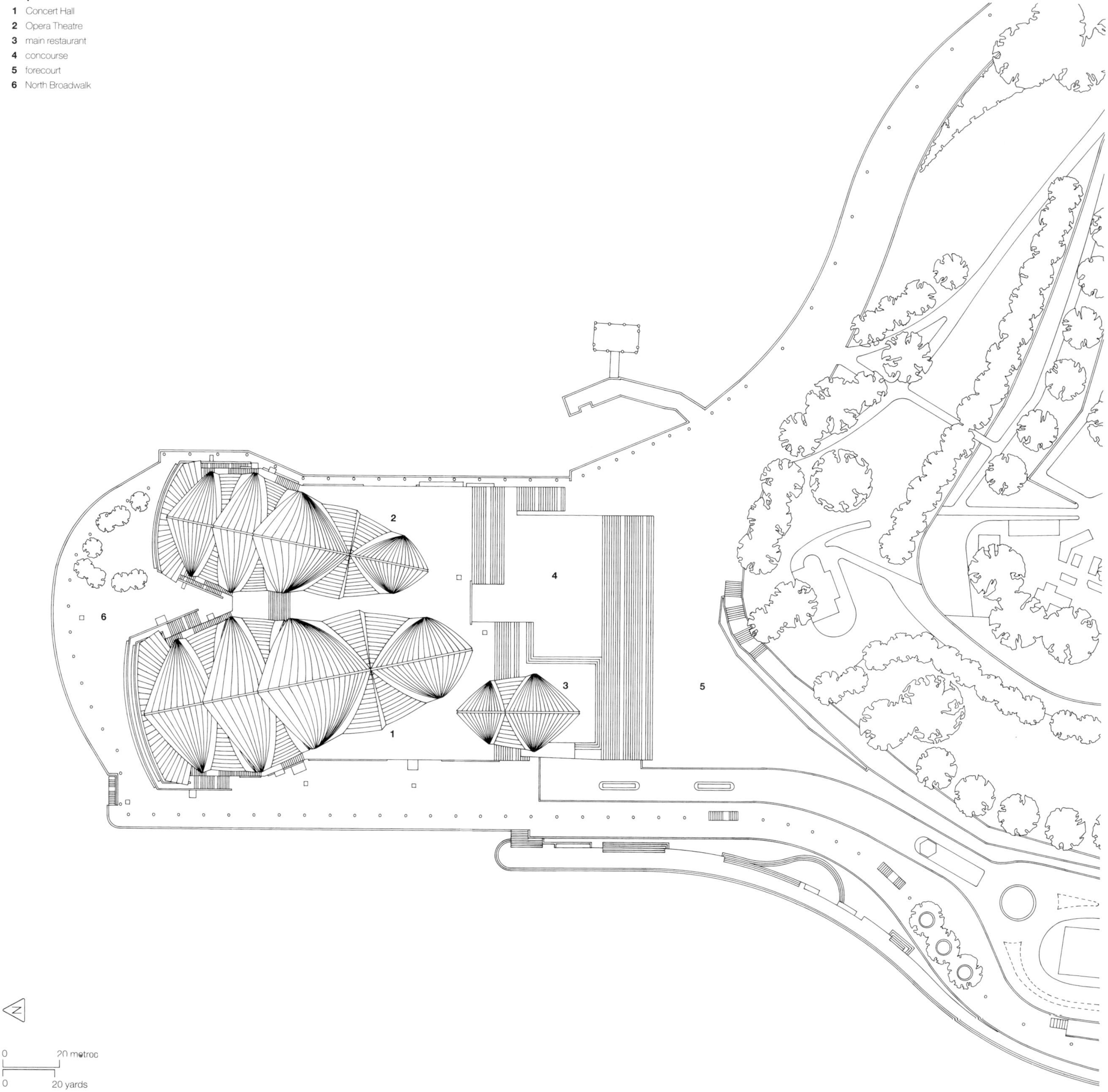
1
2
3
4
5
6
N
0
20 metres
0
20 yards

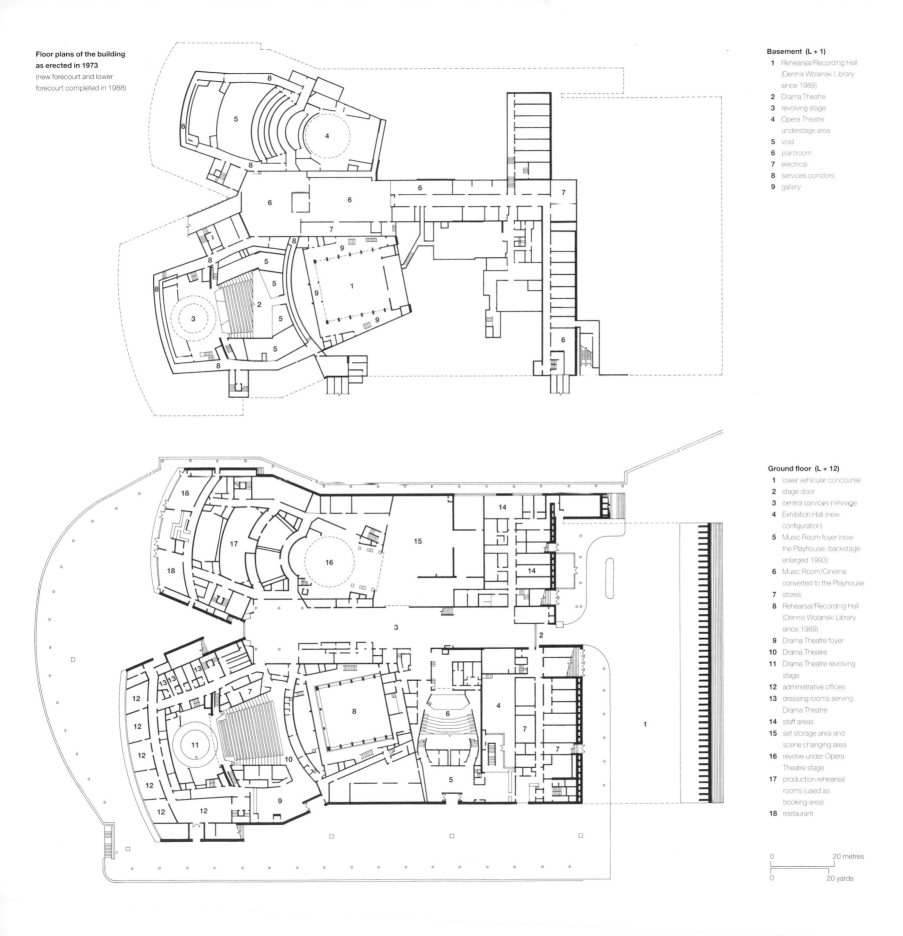

Floor plans of the building as erected in 1973
(new forecourt and lower forecourt completed in 1988)

0   20 metres

0   20 yards

Floor plans

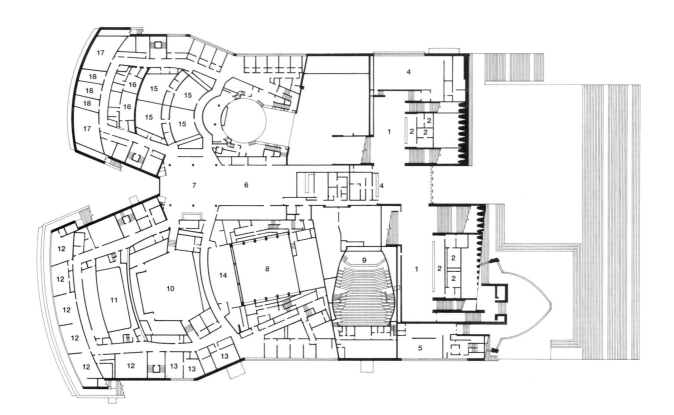

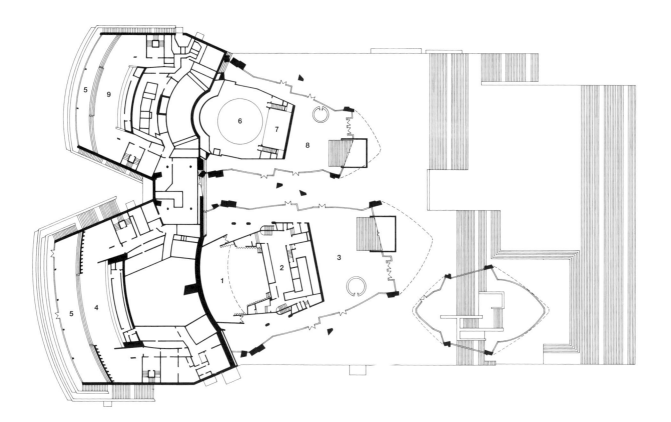

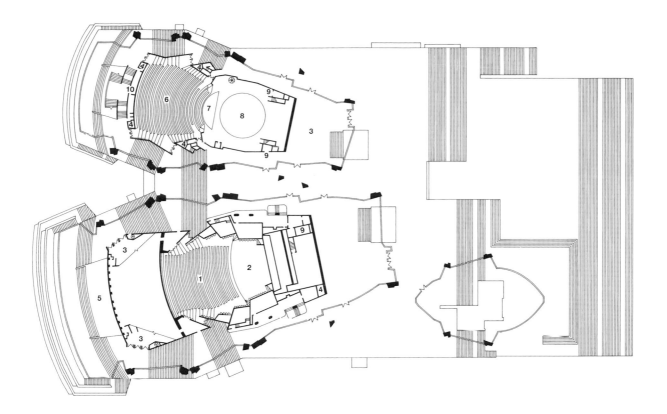

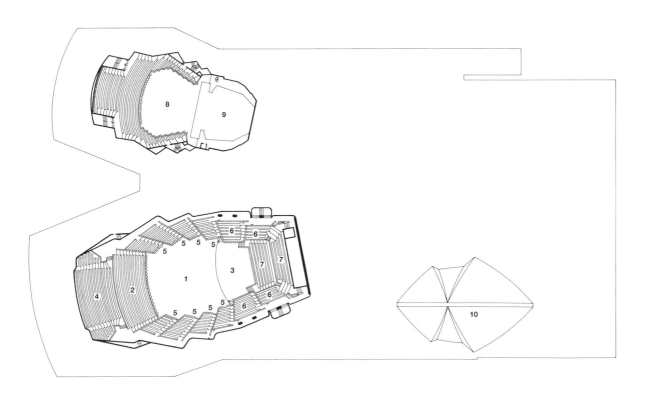

North elevation

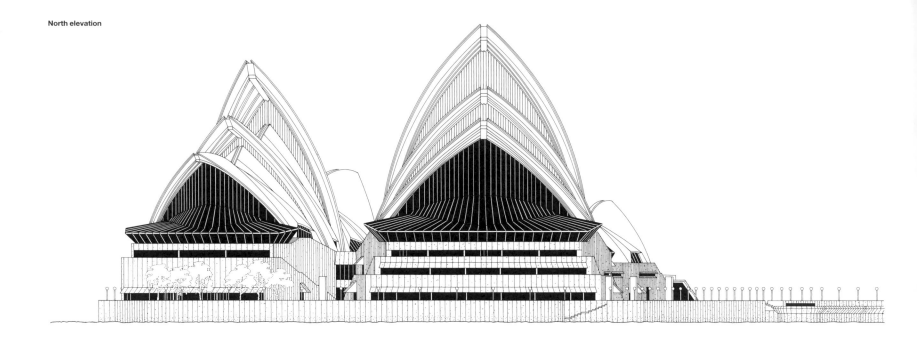

0 _____ 20 metres
0 _____ 20 yards

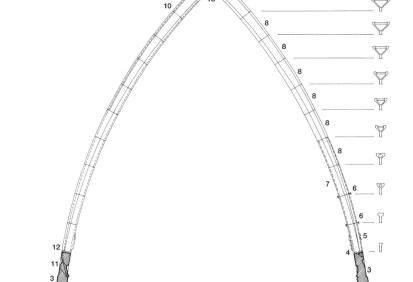

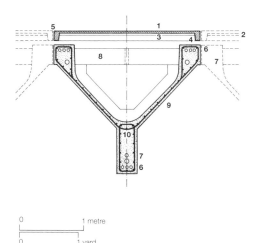

Cross-section through main shell rib segment and tile lid

1 tile surface forming 246ft 8½in radius spherical surface

2 mesh reinforced sand-cement backing to tiles

3 polyurethane foam insulation

4 reinforced concrete rib to tile lid

5 acrylic resin joint sealant

6 cable ducts for temporary stressing

7 cable ducts for permanent stressing

8 precast concrete cross bracing unit

9 precast concrete rib segment

10 mild steel reinforcing bars to rib segment

0 _____ 1 metre
0 _____ 1 yard

0 _____ 10 metres
0 _____ 10 yards

Typical tile lid detail

1 inter-rib boundary
2 stiffening ribs
3 phosphor bronze rag bolt
4 bronze sleeve

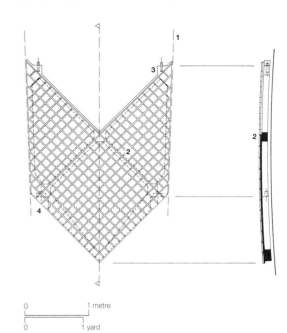

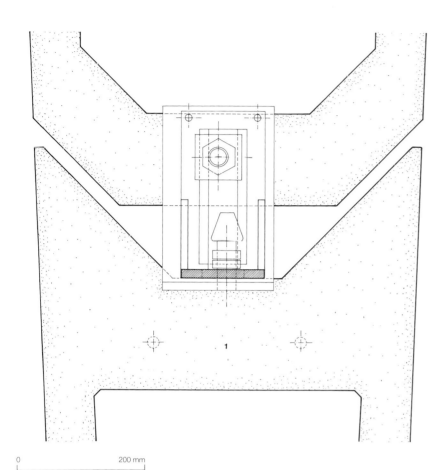

0   1 metre

0   1 yard

0   200 mm

0   8 inches

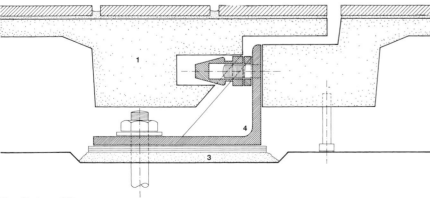

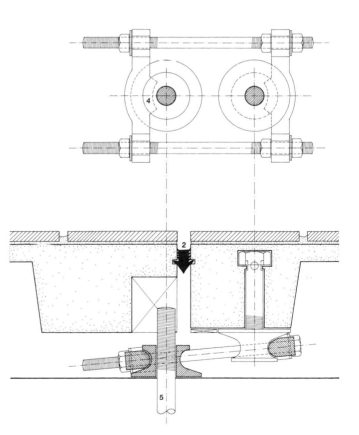

**Alternative types of tile
lid fixings**

1 tile-lids
2 seal
3 mortar bed and packing
4 bronze brackets
5 fixing bolt

North elevation and structural
system of Concert Hall glazing

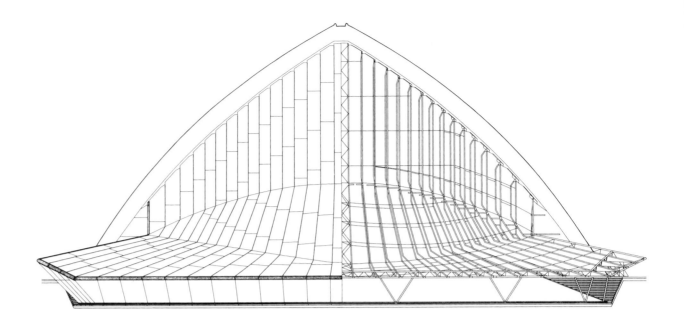

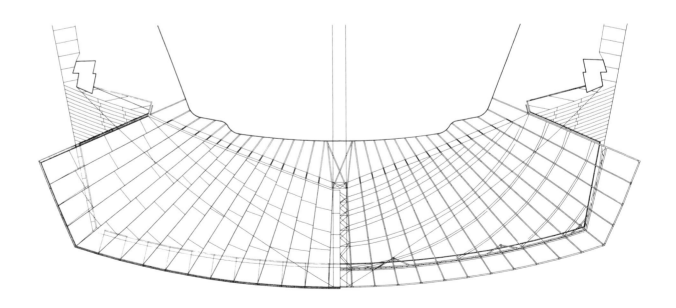

Plan view of Concert Hall glazing

0   5 metres

0   5 yards

Side view of Concert Hall glazing

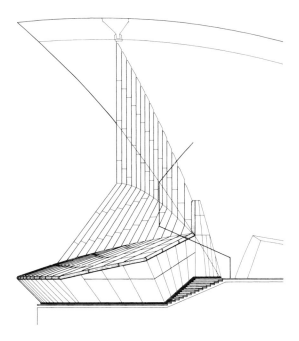

0 ─── 5 metres
0 ─── 5 yards

Nosing detail

1 centre steel tube 4⅜in
   diameter
2 bronze bracket 6ft long at
   2ft centres
3 nosing bronze extrusion
4 bronze segment, adjustable
   in width
5 standard extruded bronze
   segment
6 bronze plate 2x⅜in at 2ft
   centres
7 neoprene gasket
8 silicon rubber
9 neoprene glazing strip
10 aluminium cover strip
11 aluminium extrusion bracket
    6ft long at 2ft centres
12 continuous centre channel
    for stiffening aluminium
    louvre blades
13 aluminium channel to
    accommodate blades
14 45 degree aluminium blades
    screw fixed

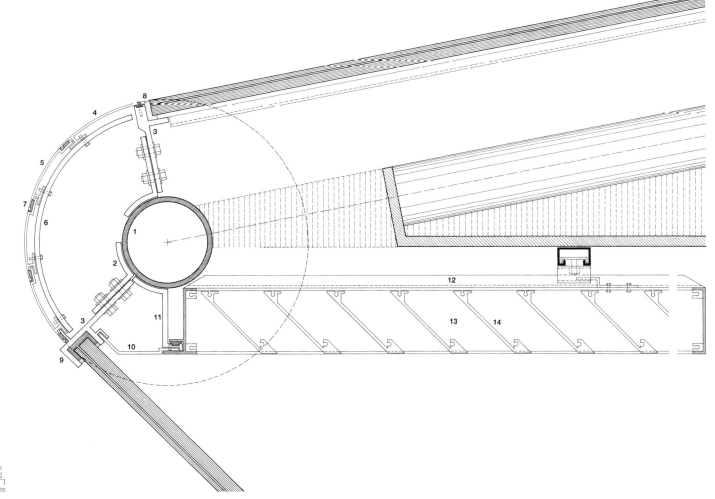

0 ─── 200 mm
0 ─── 8 inches

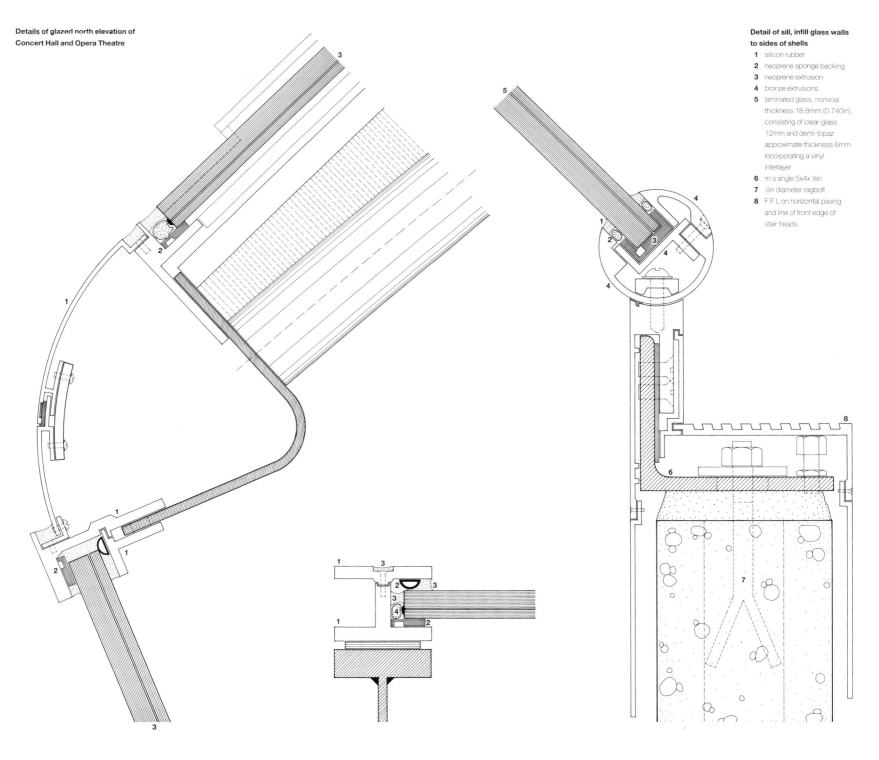

Details of glazed north elevation of Concert Hall and Opera Theatre

0   1 metre

0   1 yard

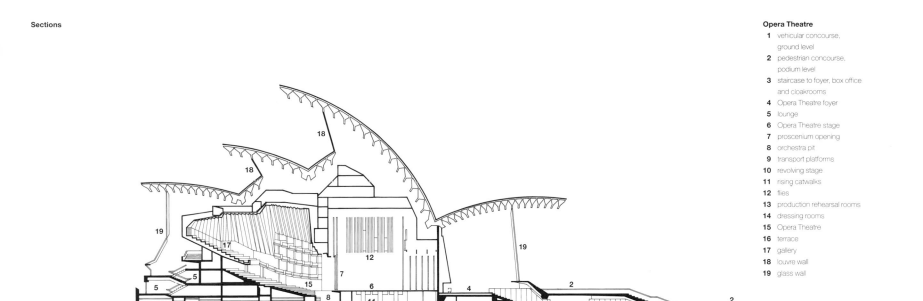

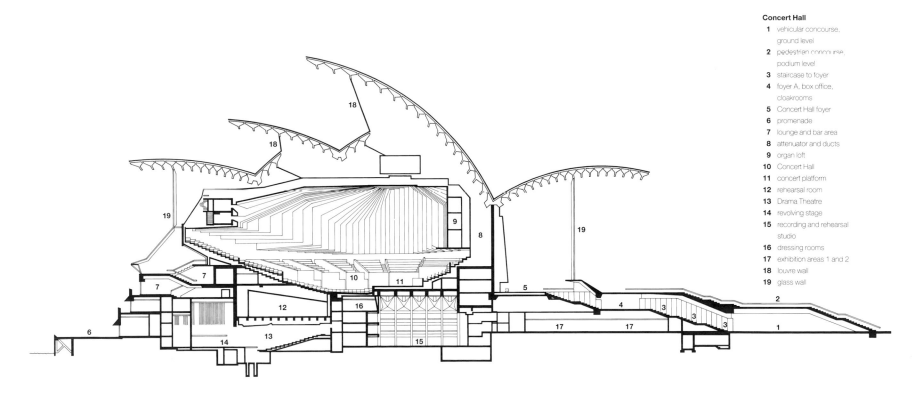

0   20 metres

0   20 yards

Author's acknowledgements

The author is grateful to John Zaat, Project Manager, Sydney Opera House Upgrade Program, and Peter Knight, Drafting Office, for supplying drawings of the fabric; Paul Bentley, Librarian, who was a perfect guide to the Dennis Wolanski Library; Christine Pike, Pictures Collection, Mitchell Library; Archives Authority of NSW; Alex Popov, private architect, who generously supplied art materials and shared his knowledge; Milo Dunphy and L Reedman, for their political perspectives; Ian MacKenzie, Ove Arup & Partners (Sydney); Eric Sierins who gave me access to Max Dupain's photographic archive; Lin Utzon for her support; and Peter Georgiades who let me read his thesis.

Illustration acknowledgements

The following illustrations have been provided courtesy of: Max Dupain: fig 4; Mitchell Library: figs 7, 8, 29–33, 37, 38, 43, 45, 48, 49. The photographs on pages 42 and 47 are reproduced with the kind permission of Peter Garrett.

Select bibliography

Documents: reports, drawings and correspondence

The Brown Book International Competition, competitions and Programme, AONSW 2/864 A–C
Competition drawings submitted by Jørn Utzon in 1956, AONSW SZ 112.
Competition Entries, AONSW 4/7930.
The Red Book, March 1958, drawings prepared by Utzon in consultation with Arup and others pub 1959, AONSW SZ 107, 1 Vol.
The Yellow Book, January 1962. Drawings by Utzon and others, presented in 1962, shows spherical section, AONSW SZ 104–5.
The Blue Book, November 1962, recommendations for car park, bus terminus, and pedestrian approach by Utzon, presented November 1962.
The White Book, February 1968, first designs by Hall Todd and Littlemore, AONSW reel 2559.
Littlemore D S, *Sydney Opera House: Anatomy of Stage Three, Construction and Completion, A General Index*. PWDNSW.
Sydney National Opera House: Structural Scheme, Stage II, 1962, Ove Arup & Partners, AONSW X995, 1 Vol.
Plans of Sydney Opera House, October 1958–June 1973, AONSW plans nos 64149–69210, X2540–816 (7,824 plans Stages I, II, III).
Stage III Standard Details 1970–72, AONSW 4/791,1.1–6.
Correspondence Mr Jørn Utzon and Mr Davis Hughes, 1 Vol, AONSW 4/7893.
Utzon v the Minister, 1957–67, AONSW 4/7896A.
Jørn Utzon Papers 1960–66, Mitchell Library, ML MSS 2362, 26 boxes and 1 Vol.
Jørn Utzon, *Descriptive Narrative*, January 1965, SOH Library.
Circular Quay Advisory Committee, Interim Report No 1: *Eastern Circular Quay*, NSW Government, November 1993.

Publications on the Sydney Opera House

Baume, Michael, *The Sydney Opera House Affair*, Melbourne, 1967.
'The Sydney Opera House', *Current Affairs Bulletin*, Vol 31, No 3, December 1962.
'Sydney Opera House', in **De Haan**, Hilde and Haagsma, lds (eds), *Architects in Competition*, London, 1988, pp136–47.
Duek-Cohen, E, *Utzon and the Sydney Opera House: Statement in the Public Interest*, Sydney, 1967.
Journal and Proceedings, Royal Society of New South Wales, Vol 106, 21 November 1973. Contains articles by P Hall, V L Jordan and M Lewis on design, acoustics and structure.
Kerr, J S, *The Sydney Opera House: An Interim Plan for the Conservation of the Sydney Opera House and its Site*, Sydney Opera House Trust, December 1993.
Norberg-Schulz, Christian, *Jørn Utzon: Sydney Opera House, Australia 1957–73*, GA, No 54, Tokyo, 1980.
Smith, Vincent, *The Sydney Opera House*, Sydney, 1974.
Sowden, Harry (ed) *Sydney Opera House – Glass Walls*, Sydney, 1972.
Yoemans, John, *The Other Taj Mahal: What happened to the Sydney Opera House*, London, 1968.

Popular and commemorative publications

Building the Sydney Opera House, the Hornibrook Group.
Hubble, Ava, *More Than an Opera House*, Sydney, 1983.
Sim, James, *Sydney Opera House, The First Decade*, Sydney, 1983.
Smith, Michael Pomeroy, *Sydney Opera House*, Sydney, 1984.
Sykes, Jill, *Sydney Opera House: From the Outside*, Sydney, December 1993.

Writings by Jørn Utzon

'Jørn Utzon: A New Personality', *Zodiac*, No 5, 1959.
'Platforms and Plateaus: Ideas of a Danish architect', *Zodiac*, No 10, 1962, pp112–140.
'The Sydney Opera House', *Zodiac*, No 14, 1965, pp48–93.
Eliel Rasmussen interview: 'Why I built the Opera House This Way', *The Sun Herald*, 13 May 1966, pp45, 67.
'Additive Architecture', special issue on the work of Utzon, *Arkitektur*, No 1, 1970, pp1–50.
'Alvar Aalto Medal 1982', Statement, Helsinki August 1982, (8 pp).
'Jørn Utzon on Architecture', *Living Architecture*, No 8, pp168–73.
'The Importance of Architects', in **Lasdun**, Denys, *Architecture in the Age of Scepticism*, London, 1984, pp214–33.

Articles on the Sydney Opera House

'Sydney Opera House, Sydney, Australia', *A+U*, Vol 3, No 10, October 1973, pp3–35.
Robin Boyd, 'The Utzon Story', *The Architectural Review*, Vol 139, No 832, June 1966, p417.
Kate Halley, 'The Harbour Swan: Fifteen years on', *Time Australia*, Vol 3, No 29, 18 July 1988, pp60–4.
Tom Heath, 'Sydney Opera House: Cathedral of Culture', *The Architectural Review*, Vol CLIV, No 919, September 1973, pp144–45.
Peter Myers, 'Une Histoire inachevée', *L'Architecture d'Aujourd'hui*, No 285, pp60–7.
Alex Popov, 'Redevelopment of Lower Concourse Level, Sydney Opera House', *Architecture Australia*, Vol 82, No 1, January/February 1993, pp50–1.
Progress Reports 1–4, in *Architecture Australia*, Vol 49, No 3, September 1960, pp69–82; Vol 50, No 3, September 1961, pp71–82; Vol 51, No 4, December 1962, pp64–77; Vol 54, No 4, December 1965, December 1965, pp72–92.
Jack Zunz, 'The Sydney Opera House', *The Arup Journal*, Vol 8, No 3, October 1973, p55.
—, 'Sydney revisited', *The Arup Journal*, Vol 23, No 1, Spring 1988, pp2–11.
Bobby Wilson, 'Sydney Opera House', *Architectural Design*, Vol XLIV, No 1, January 1974, p55.
Ying-tsao fa-shih (Treatise on Architectural Methods), edited by Li Chieh, Commercial Press, 1975.

Architects, consultants, contractors and suppliers

Location Bennelong Point, Sydney NSW 2000, Australia

Client Sydney Opera House Trust

Architects Stage I and II: Jørn Utzon; Stage III: E H Farmer, Peter Hall, Lionell Todd and David Littlemore

Civil engineers Ove Arup & Partners

Mechanical engineers Steensen & Varming

Electrical engineers Julius Poole & Gibson

Stage techniques consultant Walther Unruh

Acoustical consultant Wilhelm Lassen Jordan

Theatre planning Ben Schlanger

Quantity surveyors Rider, Hunt & Partners

Contractors Stage I: Civil & Civic Pty Ltd; Stage II: M R Hornibrook Pty Ltd; Stage III: The Hornibrook Group

Management P A Managment Consultants

Subcontractors and suppliers
air-conditioning and mechanical ventilation: Haden; balustrades/hand rails: J W Broomhead & Sons; bells: Whitechapel Bell Foundry, UK; bronze: Austral Crane; architectural bronzework: Permasteel; carpets, non-public areas: Hycraft carpet; carpets, public areas: F & T Carpets; circular stairs: Pauchet Engineering; concrete: pressure applied concrete: Nucrete; Ceilings-Timber/Oly: Cemac Brooks; electrical services: O'Donnell Griffin; electro acoustics, closed circuit television, simultaneous interpretation: Amalgamated Wireless (Asia), E P Division; fire control systems: Fire Control; hydraulic fire protection: Haden Engineering; furniture (generally): W Latchford & Sons; floors: floors, ceilings: Concert Hall floors, walls: George Hudson; floor sanding and polisher: H E Richardson; plasterboard walls, ceilings: George Hudson; Concert Hall ceiling, moulded panels: Cemac Brooks; laminated glass for glass walls: Boussoir Souchon Neuvesel; glass walls: Vascob Glass; glass wall maintenance equipment: Quick Steel Engineers; hydraulic services: J M Hargreaves & Son; lifts: Johns & Waygood; lighting: G E C Philips; stage lighting: Siemens Industries Ltd, Sydney NSW; organ builder: Ronald Sharp; painting: S A Butler; paving: precast cladding and paving: E P M Concrete; granolithic and special paving: Melocco; restaurant bars and kitchens: J Goldstein; seats-auditorium: Co-ordinated Design & Supply; stage machinery: Waagner-Biro AG (Vienna, Austria); steel work, Concert Hall ceiling: Arcos Industries; structural steel to glass walls: J W Broomhead & Sons; tiles: tiles on shell tile lids: Hoganas of Sweden; ceramic wall and floor tiling: Indent Wall & Floor Tiles; jointing tile lids: Thiocol; timber: brush box glu-lam: Allen Taylor; timber panelling: Premier joinery; dressing room joinery: Aygee.

Chronology

29 January 1957 Jørn Utzon wins first prize in Sydney Opera House competition. (Second prize, Marzella, Laschetter, Cunningham, Weissman, Brecher, Geddes & Qalls (USA); third prize, Boissevain & Osmond (UK).) Estimated cost $7M.
26 March 1958 Utzon visits Australia with Ove Arup. *Red Book* scheme submitted with halls seating 2,800, 1,200, 400 and 300.
November 1958 Stage I, foundations and podium, tender won by Civil and Civic Pty Ltd. $5.5M.
2 March 1959 Cahill and Utzon lay foundation stone.
22 March 1960 New Premier, R J Heffron, presents the Sydney Opera House Act to Parliament. Expenditure of up to $9.6M approved.
January 1963 Stage II construction of shells and tiling by the Hornibrook Group, completed in 1967. $12.5M.
March 1963 Utzon moves to Sydney. Increase in expenditure authorized to $25M.
April 1963 Stage I completed.
1 May 1965 Coalition government wins election after 24 years of Labor rule. Davis Hughes given Public Works portfolio.
25 August 1965 NSW RAIA Chapter President R A Gilling lunches with Hughes who complains about Utzon.
28 February 1966 Utzon writes to Hughes saying, 'you have forced me to leave the job'.
3 March 1966 Public protests over Utzon's dismissal.
19 April 1966 Davis Hughes appoints architecture panel to complete Opera House: Rudder, Littlemore & Rudder; Todd and Partners; and Peter Hall.
17 January 1967 Last precast shell lid in place.
28 February 1968 Stage III, contract for paving and cladding by the Hornibrook Group. $56.5M.
21 March 1967 Hughes announces no opera facilities to be provided in the Major Hall. Minor Hall changed from Drama to Opera Theatre.
March 1972 Final cost $102M ($850M in 1993 money).
20 October 1973 Official opening by the Queen.
1986 Masterplan for Circular Quay released.
8 January 1988 New forecourt and lower concourse with a covered walkway and promenade connection to Circular Quay Station completed. NSW Dept of Public Works in association with Hall Bowe and Webber. $62M.
July 1988–July 1998 30 June 1992 budget set at $103M for ten-year programme of upgrading Opera House. Revised to $111.62M in 1993.
1 August 1990 Enacon Parking builds 12 storey car park for 1,100 car parking spaces beneath Bennelong Point at cost of +$40M. Opened 17 March 1993.
8 March 1993 Plaque honouring Utzon unveiled showing spherical solution to shells.